CREATING YOUR DREAM BEDROOM

HOW TO PLAN AND STYLE THE PERFECT SPACE

CREATING YOUR DREAM BEDROOM

HOW TO PLAN AND STYLE THE PERFECT SPACE

ANDREW BANNISTER

Main Photography by Douglas Hill

STERLING PUBLISHING CO., INC.
NEW YORK

Sumptuous fabrics, in layers on the delightful bed, present a harmonious color scheme. A quilted bedcover offers a luxurious touch.

Library of Congress Cataloging-in-Publication Data Available

10 9 8 7 6 5 4 3 2 1

Published by Sterling Publishing Co., Inc.
387 Park Avenue South, New York, NY 10016

Created by Lynn Bryan, The BookMaker, London
Photography by Douglas Hill
Contributors: Lynn Bryan, with case studies written by Susan Breen and Jo Swinnerton
Editor: Kelly Ferguson

Distributed in Canada by Sterling Publishing
c/o Canadian Manda Group, 165 Dufferin Street,
Toronto, Ontario, Canada M6K 3H6

Distributed in the United Kingdom by GMC Distribution
Services, Castle Place, 166 High Street, Lewes, East Sussex,
England BN7 1XU

Distributed in Australia by Capricorn Link (Australia) Pty. Ltd.
P.O. Box 704, Windsor, NSW 2756, Australia

Printed in China

Sterling ISBN 10: 1-4027-3994-X
            ISBN 13: 978-1-4027-3994-1

For information about custom editions, special sales,
premium and corporate purchases, please contact
Sterling Special Sales Department at 800-805-5489 or
specialsales@sterlingpub.com.

CONTENTS

Part Two
Case Studies 66

A DETAILED LOOK AT SOME
UNIQUELY PERSONAL
BEDROOM SPACES

INTRODUCTION

Welcome to the leisure zone. The new-look bedroom that once featured a simple bed, a set of drawers, and a place to hang clothes is now a haven from the world with comfort as the key requirement. Descriptive words such as luxurious, tranquil, harmonious, warm, enveloping, spacious, and grand each come into your mind when you begin to imagine the dream bedroom. It is such a never-ending fantasy.

Here is a personal space where you can express yourself and push the boundaries of décor in ways you dare not elsewhere in your home. Using color in a stronger way, exploring texture and fabrics, selecting unusual surfaces and light fixtures rather than the usual suspects … these small-scale experimental exercises can give you confidence in design.

When you think of a bedroom, initially it is the bed that comes into view, for it is the dominating feature, the one thing you see when you first walk in the door. Sure, you can press a button and it will disappear into a wall if you live in a small studio apartment, but in general there is little you can do to hide the structure of a bed. Where two sleep together, what they sleep on is open for wider discussion than ever before. Electronically controlled separate mattresses can raise or lower a sleeper, pulsate the body while at rest or play. Mattresses are designed with that princess and the irritating pea spurring manufacturers on to find better ways to soften sleep.

Yet sleeping was not always so pleasurable. The four-poster bed, oh-so-desirable among those seeking romance on weekends away, was developed in Europe in the Middle Ages. A bed with four wood posts that supported a tester (made of fabric), it was designed to keep out drafts with heavy curtains hanging on all four sides. There were few window curtains at this time. However, with further improvements in insulation and draft-exclusion, the posts and tester became obsolete.

Interestingly, as you can see from the cover photograph, the four-poster bed is back in a minimalist fashion; the drapery is gone, leaving the structure on view. The fabrics have moved to the windows, which are now dressed with a view to privacy and fashion.

Opposite
The beauty of wood shines through in this impressive custom-made bedroom unit.

The most successful rooms are those that best reflect the character of the people living in them, and this is no less true of bedrooms. These days, design influences range from homegrown trends to a range of ideas and styles we saw wherever we were in the world. Mementoes of family merge with relics picked up in cities and villages in distant lands; fabric colors reflect scarves glimpsed in a marketplace, or paint colors bring back the hue of tiles on an Italian countryside roof. Artefacts from Morocco, the Caribbean, or the Far East fill space on walls where once a mirror hung—the mirror having moved out of the bedroom to the walk-in closet. Sofas, chairs, and perhaps a desk offer a place to read or e-mail friends; books on shelves and a throw for extra warmth when bed is the only place to relax. These are individual elements of a comfortable bedroom in the 21st century.

Lighting also plays a pivotal role in bedroom design. Computer systems enable us to change the mood from daylight to playful and seductive. Put that all to music and you have created the ultimate, sensual, modern boudoir for the soul.

Storage has always been an issue in the bedroom. A mere closet was just not enough. Floor-to-ceiling wardrobe doors now open to reveal strategically planned storage units, custom made for those with an extensive collection of clothes and accessories, but also well designed for the rest of us. Where space is available, walk-in wardrobes take this storage away from the bedroom, more a walk-through on the way to the ensuite bathroom.

In this book, I will take you through the processes involved in designing a bedroom, from the planning and budget stages, types of flooring, wall surfaces, lighting, and setting the style through to storage solutions for clothes and shoes and adding individual touches. In each of the sections in this book you will find both practical information and wonderful, inspirational photographs. In the Case Studies section you can see how others have designed their private spaces. It is my hope that you discover the one thing to start you on the journey to achieving your dream bedroom.

ANDREW BANNISTER

Opposite
The pale white of Gustavian-style Scandinavian bedroom furniture makes a delightful design statement. An update of the tester is above the bedhead.

PART ONE

FUNCTION AND DESIGN

THE PRACTICALS

Function is how the bedroom and its components perform their tasks. Design is how you achieve that and how it eventually looks. In the following pages we look at how to plan for both of these characteristics in your uniquely personal bedroom.

DETERMINE YOUR NEEDS

The functions of a bedroom may at first seem obvious but understanding the full function will enable you to design not only the look of the room, but also the way it needs to work for you.

What are the main functions of a bedroom?
- ▶ Sleep only
- ▶ Sleep and store all clothes, undergarments, and shoes
- ▶ Keep private mementoes
- ▶ Private place to sit and read
- ▶ Space to dress and/or apply make-up
- ▶ Space to exercise
- ▶ Home office

Ask yourself (and your partner if applicable) what makes your bedroom special. Your personal preferences will form the basis of the layout of your bedroom, so before you make any final decisions on the theme or styling, decide what the room needs to do for you and your lifestyle. The bedroom is, more and more in this modern day, a haven from the household. Here, you can escape for a few moments of tranquility, read, or watch a movie. Even sleep.

Some people prefer to exercise in the privacy of the bedroom; if that's your thing, then add space for an exercise machine to your wish list. If you like to watch late-night television or a movie, then a television riser built into the base board of your bed is a possibility. Or you can include space for a television and a DVD player in your bedroom storage unit.

THE BED

Two of the important questions are: what type of bed do you like and where do you want to place the bed?

There are many fabulous beds available, ranging from well-sprung bases and thickly padded mattresses to beds with electronic controls that fit your body in every way, ensuring a good night's sleep.

This is the most vital purchase you will make for your dream bedroom. It can also be the most expensive, depending on the level of comfort you desire, second only to the cost of storage. If the bed will be the focus of the room, such as in the case of a bed with an antique frame or an ancient, Italianate carved bed head, then it is probably acceptable to spend more on this item.

Some modern bed heads feature built-in side tables and lighting fixtures, so you will need to plan space for these, too. They are essential for individual table lamps and for storing personal items such as books and even your medication. If you like to light candles before retiring to bed, then a bedside table is more than essential.

Placing a bed ought to be a simple task, but sometimes the situation forces an unsatisfactory conclusion. A huge bed can dominate the room; a small bed can look out of place in a large room. Therefore, it is important to select a bed to fit the room's proportions. When you need more storage you could consider a bed with a base fitted with pull-out drawers (ideal for young children or teenagers). The final result will come through planning and thoughtful purchasing.

STORAGE

For clothes and accessories, a built-in, reach-in closet and a freestanding unit are among the choices. For a luxury bedroom, you can remove clothing storage to a walk-in closest or even to a separate room that is designed especially as a dressing room. For more on storage, please turn to page 46.

For other smaller items such as jewelry, books, DVDs, private papers, and other treasures, there are many individual storage opportunities, ranging from discreet shelving, and small drawers and cupboards within a larger storage unit, to small boxes made from leather, cardboard covered in fabric, natural or painted wicker, metal, and plastic.

LEISURE SPACE

Media units designed for audio and television components can be hidden away or left on display. If you want to work at a desk in the room, consider the right size for the space you will have available. Think about where it will look best in the room and make sure there is an electrical outlet close by.

The same applies to selecting and placing a sofa or small chair or a dressing table. The latter needs good natural light for make-up sessions any time of the day.

BEDROOM WISH LIST

▶ Audio-visual equipment producing surround-sound effects
▶ Bed
▶ Beautiful bed linen
▶ Ceiling treatment
▶ Central heating
▶ Chairs or sofa for casual seating
▶ Creative storage
▶ Display shelving for mementoes
▶ Drapes
▶ Dressing table
▶ Electrical outlets in convenient locations
▶ Exercise equipment
▶ Floor coverings: Wood floorboards
           Rugs
           Wall-to-wall carpet
▶ Heating: Radiator
           Underfloor system
▶ Jewelry storage
▶ Light fixtures for ceiling, walls, and bedside lamps
▶ Matching hardware styles
▶ Mirror
▶ Refrigerator for late-night cocktails
▶ Shelving for books
▶ Special mood lighting
▶ Study area
▶ TV riser
▶ Ventilation
▶ Wall coverings

DETERMINE YOUR BUDGET

The cost of everyday items for a bedroom will add up to your basic budget. Then you can add the luxuries.

The budget is by far the most important step in creating your dream bedroom. You can imagine many decorative scenarios but you must know how much each costs and then work out if you can afford to spend the money. To begin, you must determine the amount, quality, and quantity of items required for your bedroom. However, remember that although quality is often associated with higher prices, expensive items alone do not necessarily make for a better design, and that good taste and personal style do not always require a large budget. The more money you spend, the more you can do, but try not to let the budget drive the design. It is in the detail of the finishing that you see the difference between a high- and a low-budget bedroom.

Your budget consists of two elements: the purchase of products, and the cost of installation. You can further break down this latter cost into works and supplies.

The first thing is to decide how much you want to spend, and this is perhaps not as easy as you might think. If you have not taken on a project like this before, the question is: Where do you start when it comes to deciding how much you are willing to invest in the room where you sleep?

When the list is complete, examine the existing furniture and furnishings. Some of the items listed below will already exist, for example, the bed. It might be perfect for the

BASIC LIST TO START COSTING A DREAM BEDROOM

▶ Bed	Allow for cost of bed frame, mattress
▶ Headboard	Allow for cost of new headboard
▶ Bed linen, pillows, and covers	Add cost of each item
▶ Window dressings	Cost of selected curtains and blinds
▶ Flooring	Cost of selected carpets, wood, rugs, other
▶ Wall coverings	Cost of selected paint, wallpaper, and any hangings
▶ Ceiling finish	Cost of paper, paint, or fabric
▶ Lighting	Cost of fixed and standing light fittings
▶ Dressings	Cost of pictures, ornaments, and memorabilia
▶ Furniture	Cost of dressing table, chairs, bedside tables
▶ Wardrobes	Cost of fixed and free-standing storage closets
▶ Decoration	Cost of artistic painting, gilding, stenciling

new room's design, but you might want to change the bedcovers to go with the new theme. Look critically at the furniture you now own: can it be repainted or restyled? Drawers, cabinet doors, and hardware can be changed to save money. Reusing some of your existing fittings will allow you to spend on other areas.

PLAN THE DESIGN

Now you need to work out a design to follow. You can either draw the plan yourself, or contact a professional to either do it for you or help you visualize the room. Measure the walls and indicate where the doors and windows are on each wall. Also indicate the entrance to the ensuite bath, if there is one. Then measure the space your bed takes up, indicate where a free-standing or a reach-in closet is located, the chest of drawers, and any other pieces of furniture you want in the space. Using graph paper and a ruler, make a plan of your dream bedroom. Use a pencil so you can erase any errors. This activity might take some time, so set aside private time and space to do this without any distractions.

Use the list opposite to price the items you want. Use local retailers or Internet websites to build up a realistic picture of the final costs.

When you have determined what you need, the cost of renovation and installation must be considered. Changing wiring, adding media cables, repainting, buying general materials for renovation plans, adding new wood flooring and rugs or replacing carpet, or the addition of wood and other decorative panels will affect the total labor charge. For instance, do not consider handmade closets in solid hardwood if you know your budget will not stretch that far.

FEES

Labor charges are often underestimated in a project. Try not to fall into this trap. To install any item at an acceptable level of quality, you must be prepared to pay a little more than the cheapest quote, and you might have to wait for the best tradespeople. Work out the areas you are best at, and use a professional for the trades you are not quite so good at.

Depending on the type of bedroom you are creating, the following tradespeople might be needed to achieve the dream: decorator, painter, carpenter, electrician, soft furnishing supplier and installers, and craft specialists such as an artist, a fine plasterer, or a gilder.

When you have worked out a cost, add 10 to 15 percent for the unexpected. Older properties can present more surprises than newer homes. In older houses, crumbling plaster or woodwork might need replacing. If a lighting and sound system are to be added, you might have to rewire the home.

Another often-overlooked expenditure can arise when one of the family unit changes their mind! Once you see the color on a wall you might decide that it is not the right shade; or you might decide to add blinds because the sheer curtains are too sheer. These might seem like small design issues, but the cost of changes can, and does, add up to more than you expect, so add five percent for these.

PLAN THE SPACE

A successful room is the
result of planning space. Use
your list to ensure all of the
furniture will fit without
cramming it in.

You can survey the room or have it done by a
professional. Whichever way you choose to
proceed, the survey needs to be detailed,
showing every measurement around the
room: ceiling and window heights, wall
heights and widths and their types of
construction, radiator and heater positions,
light switches and fittings, electrical power
point positions, plus anything that could
possibly affect the design process. Once the
survey has been completed and a scale
drawing prepared, the design on paper or by
a computer program can commence.

Setting out what goes where will be
governed by the size of the items that need to
be fit in the room. You need to decide where
to ideally place and orient the bed, the
closets, chest of drawers, and any other items
from your dream bedroom wish list.

Think about the first thing you see when
you enter the room, because it is this that
makes the impression. This is a major point to
consider when allocating space. For instance,
it would not be wise to have a tall, blank end-
of-a-closet unit directly in view because that
would make the room feel small and dark. It is
better to first see a focal point, maybe the
bed or a view of the outside.

PLACING THE BED

A bed placed with a garden view would, to
some people, be ideal. However, this is not
always possible for people who live in urban
environments. If the bed has to face an ugly
window and view, employ decorating tricks to
make the room as bright and cheerful as
possible. For instance, use a *trompe l'oeil*
effect on a blind to create a view of your own,
or perhaps use a translucent fabric blind to
hide the view but let in the natural light.
The important thing is to have the bed in the
best position for a good night's sleep. Some
things are obvious, such as placing a bed too
close to the window or the door can mean
you sleep in a draft, and this is not good for
your body.

Experiment with sleeping directions. Lie
on the bed in all of the places it could be
placed to see which direction feels right for
you and your partner. You may be of a mind
to consult a genuine expert in Feng Shui, too.

Also ensure there is space to walk from
one side of the bed to the other. If space is
tight, make sure you can open any drawers
and closet doors without too much trouble. If
you are storing boxes under the bed, leave
space to access these with ease.

THE BEDSIDE TABLE

A bedside unit must be in proportion to the
size of the bed. In most situations, a lower
unit is preferable to one that is higher. Some
modern beds feature built-in bedside units
fitted with lighting. These are best in rooms
where space is an issue.

PLACING THE CLOSET

If the closet is to be custom fit to a wall, you should take advice from a closet designer and manufacturer. Custom-fit furniture requires consideration because where it is placed in a room can affect a plan. If the storage unit is large, it could overpower the room, so work out the correct proportion of storage unit versus the remainder of the room. Remember, dark surfaces will make a room seem smaller, so go for light surfaces. Plan its placement so the unit does not block natural light from a window.

OTHER FURNITURE

Contemporary bedrooms feature a plethora of furniture including a television, DVD player, audio system, computer, and fitness machine, as well as a desk, sofa, or chair. Also, the dressing table is now coming back in favor.

Cabinets are popular for television storage but a new hydraulic system, designed to fit into the baseboard, allows the television to rise and fall at the touch of a button, and that can save space.

If an exercise machine is required, place this away from the main foot-traffic area. In smaller bedrooms, perhaps buy a foldaway, cycle, or try yoga!

A bedroom with high ceilings can accommodate extra-tall closets, or closets with space above them to store items such as hat boxes and personal papers in neat boxes.

Controlling the space in a bedroom means that you need not trip over discarded bedcovers or feel crowded in your dream bedroom. To reiterate, the key to a happy bedroom is in planning the details.

Left
In this room you can clearly see a flow of space around the bed and through to the dressing room. The bedside tables are integral to the headboard, and are set low.

UNIVERSAL DESIGN

The purpose of universal design, a term used by architects and interior designers, is to ensure that every member of the family can safely use the facilities in an environment.

In a master bedroom the design issues revolve mainly around closets, flooring, the bed, and bedside units.

CLOSETS

When considering clothes storage, for example, it is a good idea to use components that slide back and forth, or up and down with ease. If one person is tall, the other not so tall, then consider how this situation can be made to work efficiently.

Top shelves are harder (sometimes impossible) to reach without a pair of steps than shelves placed at a lower level. One side of the closet could be made to suit a tall person; the other side, the less-tall person.

Drawers are much easier to access than low cabinets—reaching for items at the back of low cabinets can often involve bending down (not always possible when aching limbs are involved) and an awkward stance, which might cause damage to the spine and not-too-often-used muscles. If cabinets are preferred, place them at a reasonable height

from the floor. Most storage companies provide excellent catalogs with detailed measurements of pieces. (Read more about this topic in Storage starting on page 46.)

FLOORING

Safety is a major consideration in the bedroom. If the bedroom is on a different level from the passage leading to it, and you are planning a remodel, perhaps create a slope leading up from the lower level, instead of steps. For many older people, this is a good alternative.

Check for loose floorboards. These can easily be nailed down to avoid people tripping over them. The same fix-it-now rule applies to loose carpet. Tack down any edges that might be a problem.

Wood floors require a finish to protect them. Select a finish that is not slippery, especially when wet. Children might like sliding on a highly polished floor in socks, but many older people might be afraid they will slip and break a limb.

Loose rugs can also cause falls, so ensure the floor rugs are fitted with a nonslip backing material, or place a nonslip material under the rug as a precaution.

In summary, the best flooring is a nonslip surface, preferably a quality, hardwearing, fitted wall-to-wall carpet.

FURNITURE

The height of the bed is an important factor in the bedoom. If it is too high from the ground, getting out of bed in the morning might be an effort. It is better to select a bed that allows you to place your feet squarely on the floor when you are getting out of bed. A bed that is too low might cause problems because you have to bend down to get into bed, and when you want to get out of bed in the morning, more pressure is brought to bear upon the knees as you exert yourself to rise from a lower position.

Bedside units should be close enough to avoid stretching out for items placed on the surface. However, they ought to be located just far enough away so you do not bang your head on the unit if you have a night of disturbed sleep.

Unstable furniture can be dangerous to people of all ages, so fix any wobbly chair, cabinet, or table legs.

Select bedroom furniture that is easy to move around (perhaps with small wheels on each leg), and choose units designed with smooth, rounded edges rather than those with hard square corners. This type of unit (or a small desk or table) can cause bruising when people just lightly bump into it!

ELECTRICAL FITTINGS

These can wear out, so make sure new or replacement fittings are correctly installed and regularly maintained.

Trailing cables can cause serious injury by people tripping over them. It is a better idea to make sure there are enough power outlets in the bedroom so you can avoid cables to televisions, a computer terminal, and other audio or visual connections snaking across the floor.

GENERAL ADVICE

▶ Check that all bedroom windows are securely fitted and that the mechanisms are easy to open and close. Fix any broken locks or door handles.

▶ Avoid using man-made fibers for drapes and upholstery wherever possible. Natural fibers breathe and therefore do not add to any chemical mix that might already exist in the room. Another advantage: they also hang better than man-made fibers.

▶ Free-standing mirrors, often just leaned against a wall, look fantastic in modern rooms; make sure they are not likely to be knocked as people walk past.

With care and attention to detail you can make all of the bedrooms in your home safe as well as attractive.

Above
Use a hanging rail that comes down to you for heavy coats and jackets. This takes the strain out of looking after your clothes.

VENTILATION & HEATING

Getting a good night's sleep is not only the result of creating the right bedroom atmosphere. It is also the result of ensuring the air you breathe while sleeping is the purest it can be.

Some like it hot, some like it fresh, some even like it cold and snuggle up under a comforter to stay warm. No matter how you like it, you need either fresh or recycled fresh air to breathe while you sleep.

The simplest form of ventilation is an open window, but that is not always an option, especially where there is noise, atmosphere pollution, it is too hot or too cold outside, or the wind is blowing wildly and you have no option other than to shut the window tight.

Before finalizing your bedroom plan, it is advisable to consider ventilation in each of its various forms.

PASSIVE VENTILATION

This exists when you use the natural thermal properties of air to rise through vents or perhaps use the differing air pressure between inside and outside to ventilate in a similar fashion. Passive ventilation is good because it does not need electricity to run it. With no motor, there is no noise.

AIR CONDITIONING

Used to chill or heat a home, it can be expensive to run, and you can experience noise from the vents. However, in hot and humid parts of the country, a quality air conditioning system is essential for an undisturbed night's sleep.

Visit a showroom to look at the different types of units available in your price range. It is also possible to install an air conditioning unit in one room only. You can set the unit on a timer to save energy, setting it to start an hour or so before you retire to bed.

Left
A discreet vent is set into the wall
for the air conditioning system.

FILTERS

Air filters can be attached to most modern air conditioning systems to filter out pollen and other airborne particles, therefore making the bedroom more comfortable for people who are allergic to tiny dust particles that float in the air.

Stale air can contain dust, dust mites, chemical pollutants, smells, and other airborne contaminants. It can also have a higher level of carbon dioxide, which slowly replaces the oxygen as you breathe.

The amount of air you need to replace depends much on your lifestyle and the type of room or property. If you are a smoker, then you will need to replace the air more than if you don't smoke and your bedroom is large and airy. The smaller the room and the more contaminants, the more urgent the need to replace the stale and polluted air.

New furniture, man-made carpets, paint, and fittings each give off airborne solvents. A new piece of furniture that has been sprayed with paint is likely to continue to give off fumes for months. New fitted carpets can also give off fumes to begin with and provide a home for dust mites and dust when they have been in place for a while.

If you are concerned about fumes, dust, and dust mites, reduce the likelihood of these things existing in your bedroom.

CONSIDER HEAT

Depending on where in the world you live, your needs will differ. In colder climates, you will opt for warmer surface materials, and in warmer climates you will definitely opt for cooler materials. If you are determined to have stone flooring and you live in a cold climate, install underfloor heating so you get the style you desire and warmth underfoot. If the climate is hot, the cool touch of the stone becomes a blessing.

Those who live in temperate zones might choose to install wooden floors that are warm to the foot and yet cooler than carpets in the summertime.

FIREPLACES

Modern fireplace designs are better looking than they were in the past. There is nothing like a fireplace as a focal point, and as a source of heat, the open fire is second to none. Whether fueled by natural gas or by logs collected from the garden, a fireplace will add to a bedroom's attraction. It can be set at floor level or at mid-wall level, depending upon the circumstances. Check the local building regulations before buying a fireplace to ensure it can be installed without much structural alteration.

HEAT EXCHANGERS

A process that extracts the warm, stale air from your bedroom and passes it through a heat exchanger. The stale air heats the cool fresh air as it passes back into your home via another pipe. This is an efficient way to save on heating bills as the systems are between sixty to eighty percent efficient. The cost of the energy to run them is less than the cost of heating cold air via your heating system.

SETTING THE STYLE

Some people have a clear idea of how they want the bedroom to look, while some do not know where to start the process of setting a bedroom style.

Style ideas can be culled from anywhere, including magazines, catalogs, interior design books, and movies. One of the new influential styles is the hotel bedroom style, which has grown from more and more of us visiting modern spa hotels at home and in far-flung exotic countries. Replicating the style of a hotel room that made us feel comfortable has become a big trend. You learn from hotel designers, who have a restricted space in which to impress us. You can also sleep on the same mattress as you did during your stay, as many hoteliers realize the potential from sales of their well-made mattresses.

A visit to bedroom showrooms and interior design companies, where you can view furniture, colors, fabrics, and accessories, will give you more ideas. This is a good way to discover styles that perhaps you had not previously considered.

Here are some simple rules to apply when selecting a style.

Decide the general design criteria you want for the bedroom:

- ▶ Light and airy
- ▶ Dark and moody
- ▶ Soft and subtle
- ▶ Cool and calm
- ▶ Bright and colorful
- ▶ Monochromatic
- ▶ Minimal
- ▶ Elegant
- ▶ Modern
- ▶ Traditional
- ▶ Cultured
- ▶ Themed
- ▶ Distinctive

It is a good idea to write down the exact words that describe what you want because these will be integral to creating the basis of your design. The words and phrases should encapsulate the essence of your chosen theme. They should set the scene and be your guide throughout the design process.

If you selected the word "elegant," you need to elaborate what you mean by elegant. You can do this by cutting out images you think meet the elegant criteria from home interior magazines and placing them, alongside the word, on a large sheet of white cardboard. Then place samples of colors and fabrics that you like, plus the styles of furniture and soft furnishings, alongside the tearsheets.

Gradually, you will build up a picture of the bedroom style. Interior designers do a similar exercise, creating a mood board. It sets the scene and gives you opportunities to ensure you make the right decisions.

However, it is not practical to carry a large piece of cardboard around with you, so write down your key words on a small piece of paper, and keep it handy to remind you of what you are trying to achieve. This focus will, hopefully, prevent you from wandering off the chosen track. It is easy to be distracted from your style theme, especially when you see so many attractive products that, although wonderful in their own right, will probably be wrong for your style. Keeping a focus on your goals is paramount.

If you decide upon a period theme, for instance Retro or Art Deco, you need to research that design period, familiarizing yourself with fabric and furniture designers working during that time, as well as the predominant colors used for paints and accessories. This exercise is essential in creating the entire look in your bedroom.

Above
The Asian theme is obvious from the first moment you see the sliding doors and the rush matting on the floor.

Opposite
Soft furnishings in hues of the same neutral color make this rich style statement.

Other themes based on the style of a country you may have visited, such as Africa, can be replicated using the same research methods. The photograph opposite shows an African theme authentically recreated .

Interestingly, sometimes you can discover that the theme you selected is not for you! If this happens, then perhaps you did not do enough research at the start, so make sure you choose carefully and that the style is right for your home.

COLOR & STYLE

Color sets a style and a mood in any room, but in a bedroom it is vital to select the right color. Avoid using bright colors if you desire a calm mood, and use soft tones instead.

As in fashion, there is a cycle in color trends. You will note a color or combination of colors seen in clothes stores makes its debut in accessories for the home soon after. If you are someone who likes to follow fashion, and cost does not matter, then it is best to work with a plain background and accessorize with the latest colors, using them in bed linens, cushion covers, and drapes.

If you are not a fashionista, do not fear. Certain colors are classic; time and time again they are seen in homes that range in age from one to more than a century. Classic colors include all shades of white, black, brown, blue, and red. The secret to long-lasting style is in how you use the colors.

Remember, too, that some colors are just too feminine for a male partner or husband to feel comfortable with when they are in a bedroom. Shades of blue, from dark navy to pale duck-egg blue, are unisex bedroom colors, as are red, orange, brown, and neutral colors. Avoid pink at all costs for adults.

If you are unsure of color, use the color wheel to help determine which colors fall into a similar tonal area.

Always test a paint color on a bedroom wall. However, painting a little patch in the middle of a large wall will not help you see how the color will look in a large space. This is because the surrounding color of the existing wall affects the way you see the color. Paint an area of at least 30" (75cm) square to get an idea of the true effect.

Small patches of deeper color on an expanse of a pale background make the smaller area seem much darker than it will look when you paint the entire room. My advice is not to hurry this color selection process, look at the patches at various times of the day, and be firm about your decision.

GENERAL ADVICE

Avoid seeking too many opinions. It's not that you don't appreciate input, but the wrong advice can sway you from your decisions. You have no doubt experienced those moments when you are happy with something but make the mistake of asking a friend what they think! Their comment can shatter your vision.

Be careful not to "overdesign" the bedroom. Many people feel they need to keep adding more furniture and accessories, more design detail, and more lighting to create perfection but, remember, it is true that sometimes less is a lot more.

Opposite
Reminiscent of Africa, this bedroom is a stunning example of a well-designed room based on a theme.

S U R F A C E S

Tactile, sensual surface materials add a subtle level to the design of any room, and especially the bedroom. In this section we look at surfaces for walls, window and ceiling treatments, and floor surfaces.

WALLS

Walls are the largest expanse to decorate in a bedroom. They present endless opportunities to be creative in all of the senses.

It is an exaggeration to say nearly all bedroom walls are painted or papered, but the truth is, most are! Yet, there are many other types of wall coverings and finishes which you will find described in this chapter.

The important thing is to select a finish suitable to the style and finished effect you desire, and not to be constrained by what is considered the usual thing to do. Following is a list of favorite finishes for bedroom walls.

PAINT

Paint remains the most popular finish for bedroom walls. Traditionally, one color, or a combination of two or more colors, adorns the walls and ceiling, providing a backdrop for a style provided by furniture and soft furnishings. A matte or silky sheen finish is the best for walls, with a high-gloss finish on doors, door surrounds, and other surfaces such as window frames.

Paint can also be used in decorative ways. Bagging, ragging, stippling, dragging, stenciling, and marbling are just some of the effects you can achieve. An effective paint finish for a relaxing mood is a light wash all over the wall, giving a soft hue to the room. An artist can bring walls to life, whether you want artistic scenes depicting views of rolling countryside or a fantasy future world.

One of the new trends for painted surfaces is a metallic finish with soft silver, copper, and gold among the colors for use either as a feature wall or on all four walls. The other trend is for eco-friendly paints that do not contain too many chemicals. Ask your local paint store expert what is best for you.

WALLPAPER

Wallpapers are fashionable again, but not as you knew them. New additions to the paper collections include papers with vinyl, fabric, embossed, hand-printed, flock, foil (in both matte and shiny finishes), and cork surfaces.

Above
Strong color on the walls suits this teenager's room.

Above

Interior designer Claudia Aquino has created the essence of eclectic style in this bedroom, with a nod to modernity in the transparent stool at the bottom of the bed and the luscious silken fabric bedcover.

Silk wallpapers have been used for centuries but are now greatly improved, as are the types of wallpaper pastes and adhesives used to adhere the new papers to the wall.

Highly textured wall coverings, made possible with the latest technologies and materials, are the basis of this new movement in wall finishes. Perhaps the time has come to be bold again with special foiled patterns, or be subtle with delicate textures. It depends on the mood you wish to create in your bedroom. Most stores give you a sample to take home and pin onto the wall so you can get an idea of whether the pattern is too big for your room, or lost on the wall.

For a large-patterned wallpaper, all other furnishings must be as bold so they do not get overwhelmed by the pattern. If you love a specific large pattern, but feel it will be too much on every wall, use it as a feature wall behind a bed, or on the wall opposite the bed. Choose a color from it and make that the color of the room's acccessories.

FABRIC

Whether you glue fabric panels directly onto the walls, stretch the fabric over a frame of light battens, or line the fabric with batting or fire-resistant foam, fabric can look fantastic in bedrooms. It helps deaden sounds from inside or outside the home, resulting in a wonderful, calm atmosphere.

A wide selection of fabrics are suitable for use as a wall covering. Cotton, calico, silk, satin, lace, woven wool, linen, man-made, and hessian are ideal. The key is to use a fabric with body, so it does not sag when in place.

POLISHED PLASTER

Polished plaster provides a colorful finish that does not (usually) need repainting. Developed by Italian decorators who mixed marble dust and pigments, it can achieve many different effects. Polished plaster finisheson a wall can be smooth, glossy, or matte.

WOOD PANELING

This is a traditional wall covering made modern by the use of exotic woods (use only wood from sustainable forests). Natural wood and laminated wood surfaces can often be indistinguishable from each other, so if cost is a problem, and you want the effect, search around for a laminate that looks as good as the real thing. The grain of each piece of wood is the major attraction; the more beautiful the grain, the more impressive the wall feature will be. When selecting panels, try to match the grain and the color of each piece with the next to keep the appearance consistent. Remember that dark wood will make a small room seem dark; instead use a wood with a light finish in a small room.

Below
Grainy wood panels make an impressive wall feature.

METALLIC MATERIALS

Use quality gold leaf or silver foil sheets on specific walls for a glamorous effect in a bedroom, especially if you desire to have a different look. You could cover all the walls, as in the case study on page 112.

As previously mentioned, try a paint with a metallic finish on the ceiling or as a feature wall. Add the design element of a color-changing light sequence, and you will see effects you would not have dreamed possible.

MIRROR

Visually expand the height, width, and depth of your bedroom with the use of wall mirrors. Large mirrored panels work wonders to reflect natural and artificial light or bring a beautiful outdoor view into the room. Since light levels differ dramatically throughout the day, experiment by placing a small mirror on a section of wall for a few days to get a better understanding of how the mirror will have an impact on the space. For example, placing a large mirror opposite a window will amplify daylight but may also create a blinding glare during certain times of the day.

Mirror panels are manufactured with a variety of edge finishes, including plain and beveled. Mirror surfaces can be antiqued to suit a traditional room. This look is popular in replicating period French style.

If you plan to invest money in a wall-sized mirror, hire an experienced glazer to do the installation. Mirrors are costly and fragile; in the end, you will save money and time by hiring a professional.

UNUSUAL FINISHES

These include leather and suede, bamboo, colored glass, back-lit glass, and smooth concrete. You can cover a wall with leather in much the same way as you would use a fabric, which is ideal for a masculine bedroom look. Select a dark color, because despite your best efforts, both leather and suede will mark easily.

Bamboo products are popular because of the desire to use sustainable materials. This material can be used in the same way as other wood paneling. One benefit is that bamboo is light in color and light in weight, and it is a natural product so it will be good for your health, too.

Colored and back-lit glass walls are suitable for use in the design of a modern bedroom. The main advantage of a glass wall is that it lets in light and makes a space seem larger than it is. Technology has developed greatly in the past decade, and much of the glass developed for use in large, commercial buildings is being used in newer domestic architecture, even as an adventurous floor and to build staircases.

Toughened glass can be sandblasted, etched, or used plain in fixed or movable sliding walls. Glass is very effective when you want light to reach areas that might otherwise remain dark for most of the day.

Glass bricks, which have been around for decades, can look fantastic as a wall.

Automatic lighting systems add another design feature to a glass wall. Set the system to a calming color sequence, and you will drift off to sleep bathed in a soothing light.

WINDOW TREATMENTS

For a complete look, select the style of the drapes or blinds with consideration to the theme of the bedroom. Do not skimp on fabric.

Window dressings are most important in a bedroom. It may be that you will not always want the morning or afternoon sun to shine across the bedroom, but it would be great if you could sometimes use the natural light to add atmosphere without switching on the artificial lights.

Drapes and blinds are the answer to controlling how much light can enter a room. Consider how light passes through the various types of window blinds and drapes when thinking about how to create privacy. Some fabrics allow light in and also provide privacy, but take advice from professionals or you might find that your window fabric keeps the room private in daylight, but might allow people to see through the window treatment at night as they walk past.

When looking for fabric to add a finishing touch there are all sorts of practical aspects to consider. The thickness of a curtain fabric is important because it will have an effect on the way the fabric hangs. Also, there are other thicknesses you can add to drapes, such as linings and interlinings, to keep out the cold, and reduce exterior noise levels and the amount of street light that shines in.

Left
Sheer fabric makes a soft impressions as curtains across a large expanse of windows.

CURTAINS

Some curtains or drapes are closed at night, and others are there just for effect; it depends upon your style.

Voiles and semitransparent drapes affect the way the light enters the bedroom. If you live on a busy street but like the idea of this type of drape or blind, perhaps use a roller blind made of black-out fabric that can be rolled up during the day, out of sight, and pulled into place during the night.

There are a number of elegant effects that can be created just by draping voiles over a rod placed across a window, perhaps leaving them to pile in a heap on the floor.

Linen, jute, pure cotton, and satin-finish fabrics make up well as both roman shades and drapes. Silk, satin, metallic, and damask fabrics are perhaps more suited to drapes.

Plain or patterned fabrics? This is a common dilemma, one which is solved by a good look around the room. If the walls are busy, go for a plain fabric, and vice versa.

Window dressings need not match the bedcover. Instead, select a color from the bedcover and repeat that in drapes and other accessories. It can be a shade or two lighter or darker and be in a different texture. To achieve a tranquil mood in the bedroom, use matching hues rather than contrasting colors. It is easier to match wall, floor, and ceiling colors to a fabric than the other way around.

In bedrooms with an entire wall of windows or where the windows are different heights and widths, you could consider dressing the entire wall (floor to ceiling, wall to wall) with one curtain set. Use a strong pole and several sets of brackets, to hang three separate curtains.

BLINDS

Blinds are excellent for those who want a simple treatment at the bedroom window. There are different types of blinds to choose from, including venetian, roman, Austrian, roller, combined roller/venetian, bamboo, grass, vertical, metallic, and blackout as well as see-through fabric blinds that rise up, not roll down, in the window frame.

SHUTTERS

These can be hung on the exterior or inside. You can choose from roller shutters, louvre shutters that can be adjusted by a rod on the shutter, and electric security shutters. There is a wide choice of finishes and styles. Painted, wooden, metallic, and plastic products are available and each has its own style appeal and benefits.

CURTAIN EQUIPMENT

A wide range of poles and finials, used for a final decorative touch, is at your fingertips. Made of brass, steel, iron, wood, or bamboo, poles and their supports make a statement.

If you are going to hang curtains from a pole, you can choose a curtain with large or small eyelets, fabric strips that tie into bows, or fabric straps that slip through a pole. Rings made in various sizes and materials can be attached to curtain tape or sewn directly onto the curtain, then attached. Make sure the style of the pole or track matches your décor.

Curtain tracks are usually hidden behind the curtain heading or can be hidden by a pelmet or a valance. Track materials range from plastic to metal and aluminium.

Traditional pelmets, either painted or covered with fabric, are again making an appearance in bedrooms, as are steel tension wires to which you clip small curtain rings.

A successful window treatment is one that is hardly noticed yet without it, the room appears naked.

Opposite
A pelmet runs across the top of the expanse of window. Blinds are also fitted to control the amount of light that enters.

CEILINGS

Some of you have a clear idea of how they want the bedroom ceiling to look, while others will hardly know where to begin the process of decorating such heights.

The ceiling is often called the fifth wall and is an integral part of your room's design. You can treat a ceiling in the same way that you treat a wall, although there are a few practical and obvious differences. However, the ceiling need not remain a dull, blank canvas of paint.

The tented ceiling, once popular in the 1960s, can hide a thousand idosyncracies, but it might not be good for people with dust allergies. Instead, you could cover the ceiling with a leather-look material. There are various surface materials that look like leather (vinyls) that can be applied with a special adhesive. Suede-effect material is applied the same way or by using suede surface paints. The ceiling is also the perfect place to use a soft, metallic paint in silver, bronze, gold, or any hue you adore. Combine the paint effect with flattering lighting, and the ceiling could look absolutely sensational.

Color on the ceiling plays a major role in how a room looks. Use a dark color on a ceiling, and it will visually lower the height of the ceiling; paint it a light color and it will appear higher than it is. This is important in a small room. Although, sometimes using dark colors in a small room can help with the mood.

Mirrored ceilings are acceptable again, especially above a four-poster bed. It can create a very intimate mood because the bed is enclosed by hanging drapes which, along with the bed linen, are reflected in the mirror, creating a snug environment.

Left
A fantasy in white: the stage is set with feathers and voile.

Left
Wood ceiling
beams and a steel
beam are in stark
contrast to the
white ceiling
panels with their
gloss finish.

Texture can be added to a ceiling by adding plain or patterned wallpaper, plaster effects, stamped-tin ceilings, and fabric. In many cases, adding a texture can hide small defects in a ceiling that is perhaps not quite as level as you would like. However, texture, if used in a bedroom where space is an issue, will make the room look smaller.

Decorative touches for your ceiling could include coving and plaster reliefs, such as a ceiling rose, in a traditional decorating scheme. You can also produce an amazing effect by splitting the ceiling levels, then adding perimeter light that causes the walls, around where they meet the ceiling, to glow. This effect can be on a timer so every now and then the colors and intensity of the light can change the mood.

You could also lower the ceiling over the bed, adding lighting effects, to replicate the look of a four-poster bed. Or, just keep the ceiling plain white and throw projected light or still (or moving) images across the ceiling as the mood takes you. (Read more about lighting and the wonderful effects you can plan starting on page 58.)

TIP TO FILE AWAY

Here is a most important lighting tip. It is a small but enlightening gem. A ceiling treatment needs light thrown up at it, rather than light falling down from it. Avoid filling the ceiling space with downlighters. Use up lighting or side lighting instead of downlighters.

FLOORS

Choosing a floor for your
bedroom will depend on its
location within the home, the
type of architecture, and your
own personal preferences.

A bedroom floor is just like any other floor in
your home. Use the style of the bedroom as a
starting point to narrow the flooring choices,
which can be more in tune with the owner's
personality because of the intimate nature of
the sleeping space.

Flooring options vary enormously from
old planks and new wood, to carpet, bamboo,
glass, concrete, limestone, sandstone, slate,
granite, marble, and any composite material.
Rugs (handmade or manufacturered) have a
role to play on wood or stone floors, too.

As one of the dominant design elements
in the room, the floor must work with other
components to express the overall aesthetic.
For example, wide oak planks paired with an
antique brass bed connotes early 20th-
century style, while a sleek, stone floor
suggests a contemporary look; when mixed
with mahogany cabinetry it crafts a classic,
timeless look.

In open-plan master bedrooms with
distinct zones for sleeping, dressing, and
relaxing, many interior designers use a
change of flooring to delineate the function
areas of each of the spaces. You might
consider a wood floor accented with a large
rug for your bedroom, and a carpeted area in
the adjacent dressing room. The different

surfaces will provide a useful contrast, and
delineate the areas well.

However, when the room is connected to
a bathroom area or a sitting room, you can
use the same type of flooring to create a
streamlined look, and provide a smooth
transition between the two spaces.

Finally, allow your bedroom budget to
steer you toward the affordable choices in
flooring. Use accurate room measurements to
gather quotes on materials, costs, and labor,
and be sure to have drawings in hand to
show the placement of large fixtures such as
the bed, the closet, a sofa, a dresser, or other
freestanding or built-in furniture.

A footnote to those with small-sized
bedrooms: Limited square footage works to
your advantage when in comes to choosing
your dream material. Pricier floor treatments
can be surprisingly affordable.

HARDWOOD

The warmth of a natural wood floor enriched
by nature's grain, gleaming from the added
benefit of a wax coating, has timeless appeal
and is suitable for many decorating themes.
However, you should install wooden flooring
from sustainable forests.

Wood species such as oak, ash,
chestnut, beech, and walnut are all suitable.
Pine is a softwood and will dent more easily
than other woods. Bamboo flooring is a new
type of eco-flooring, as is a recent product
made from rubber tree wood.

Pros: Wood is popular thanks to the latest
generation of polyurethane sealants. Milled in
an assortment of tones, grain patterns, and

Opposite
Hardwood
flooring is
ideal in a
simply
decorated
bedroom.

plank widths, the natural beauty of wood creates a warm contrast with other materials. Wood floors may be sealed onsite or installed in prefinished planks.

Cons: The longevity of wood is determined by the quality of sealer used. Hardwood surfaces require periodic sanding and then resealing to keep up a good appearance and can show signs of wear in high-traffic areas such as doorways.

Wood floor finishes include oiled, waxed, varnished, painted, limed, stained, or bare and untreated.

LAMINATE

Pros: Laminate offers durability and easy maintenance and is made up of a solid core beneath a realistic photograph of wood or stone, topped with a strong, clear plastic layer. It cleans up with soap and water and retains its excellent appearance even in high-traffic areas. It is less likely to warp or twist (a common problem with wood, especially if there are seasonal variations in humidity).

Cons: As an engineered product, laminate lacks the authentic character of natural materials such as hardwood, carpet, and stone. In addition, depending upon the depth and thickness of the sub floor, laminate floors can sound hollow when you walk on them.

BLOCK/PARQUET FLOORING

Pros: Parquet flooring is made of small, solid sections of hardwood set into a variety of patterns, such as herringbone. Popular in the early 20th century, it is returning as an underfoot feature. Also, patterns can be made with different-colored parquet wood.

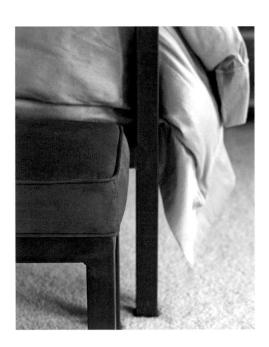

Far Left
Softly textured carpet tones with the bed linen.

Left
Sophisticated matting sits on a polished floor.

Cons: This can look great in bedrooms but it can be expensive to design and lay. If laid in a heated environment, the parquet blocks can dry out unless they are well maintained.

TILE

Pros: Tile types range from porcelain, stone, ceramic, terra cotta and mosaic, and offer design flexibility in a bedroom. They are ideal in hot climates, but not so ideal in cold climates, although a tile floor with underfloor heating could work well. Easy to install and available in an array of shapes, sizes, colors, and styles, tile is easy to customize to a number of applications. Properly maintained tile floors will survive heavy wear and tear.

Cons: For safety, low-sheen, skid-resistant tiles approved for use as flooring should be considered, especially if the bedroom has an ensuite bathroom.

CONCRETE

Pros: Waterproof and durable, decorative concrete is a practical surface with a unique look. Generally poured on site into a pre-built frame, concrete floors can be tinted, stained, etched, and even embedded with smooth bits of glass or rock to create a custom appearance suited to modern bedrooms.

Cons: Concrete is a cold, hard surface that can make a space appear harsh and austere if not mixed with other warm design elements. Depending upon the finish chosen, sealing and polishing may be required to maintain the surface. Concrete flooring is pricy and labor intensive. In rare cases where the surface does not set properly, the entire process must be repeated to get satisfactory results.

CARPET

Pros: Made from wool, silk, nylon and other man-made fibers, carpets come in a variety of colors, textures, thicknesses, and qualities. Carpets can be laid wall to wall, set as a centerpiece on a wood floor, or be made as an individual rug design.

Cons: For those who suffer from asthma, use of a flooring material that can hold dust and mites, such as a fitted carpet, should be kept to a minimum.

OTHER FLOORING TYPES

Natural flooring which includes woven grass, sisal, coconut, coir, jute, and seagrass.

Cork which comes in various finishes, such as pre-sealed, vinyl coated, or bare and is also available in differing types of cork and stained colors.

Stone which includes limestone, granite, and marble. It is hard-wearing, cool in hot climates, but for temperate and colder climates it is best to install underfloor heating. Stone can be laid in differing ways: square or oblong slabs can form patterns, and by using smaller sections you can make images, or other decorative designs. Stone can be laid in a pre-polished form, or polished on the floor after laying.

Glass which is reinforced is more popular as designers push the boundaries. Glass panels, lit from under, add a different dimension to a bedroom floor.

STORAGE

Whether you have the space for a full walk-in closet or just a wall of reach-in closets, storage is the most important feature in your bedroom. Clothes, accessories, and favorite items need a home, and the correct arrangement solves everything. Look inside and see how many options you have.

STORAGE TRENDS

You know you have far too many clothes and accessories, with boxes and chests of drawers overflowing with those old favorites. Now is the time to de-clutter your life and plan a closet to die for.

Left
A pull-out trouser rack makes it easier to find the right pair quickly.

Below
Custom-made storage in this luxury bedroom includes a leather and wood stool that doubles as a serving tray for drinks and hot chocolate.

The first task facing you and your family in planning bedroom storage is to make a detailed list of how you currently store your clothes, accessories, and small favorite items. Then use the list to help you estimate how much more or less you need in the new bedroom design.

A sense of order provides a calm state of mind. To have a sense of order, you have to be on top of the clutter in your bedroom. This requires you to face up to the fact that the outfit you wore ten years ago is not going to look as good now. Or ever again. And, those shoes with dented high heels are no longer cool. It's hard, but you must do this: throw them out. Ask a friend to help you decide which clothes to throw out, which to give to charity, and which to keep.

Any soft, cuddly toys of any size, if you are an adult, should be banished from the bedroom, too, unless they are for use during the nighttime visits of small children.

When you have sorted through the excesses, you can begin the real work.

To assist in planning, sort clothes into three categories as below by measuring the length of clothes to be hung on rails.

Short
Trousers (pants)   Skirts
Jackets   Shirts
Blouses   Slacks

Medium Long
Jackets
Mid-length dresses (below the knee)

Long
Full-length day dresses
Coats (summer and winter weights)
Trousers (pants) hung by hem or waist
Evening dresses

WOMEN
Shirts and blouses: 35" to 40" (89cm to 101cm)
Short dresses and pants hung by the cuff or waistband: 48" to 50" (121cm to 127cm)
Coats and evening dresses: 60" to 70" (152cm to 178cm)
Skirts: 38" to 42" (96cm to 106 cm)
Pants hung folded: 20" (50cm)

MEN
Shirts: 40" to 45" (89cm to 114cm)
Pants hung folded: 20" (50cm)
Blazers: 38" to 42" (96cm to 016cm
Pants hung by the cuff or waistband: 48" to 50" (121cm to 127cm)

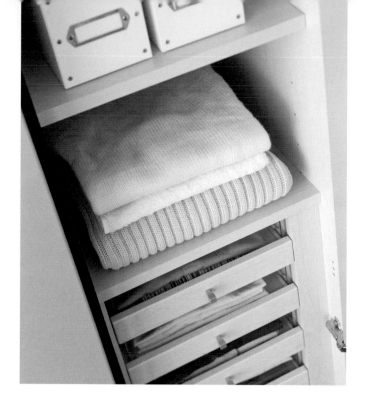

Measure how much rail you are currently using for each of the above. For example, you may find that most of the rail length is being used for short items, and there is plenty of unused space between the bottom of the garments and the lower part of the wardrobe. Then estimate how much rail you will need for the future. Apply the same detailed approach for each length. Use the information gleaned from this exercise to build your closet.

STORAGE NEEDS
You now need to establish what else requires storage in your bedroom:

HIS
Underclothes   Socks
Shoes   Ties
Belts   Hats
Scarves   Watches & jewelry

Add a small set of drawers or a countertop above a chest of drawers for the things you

Above

Sweater storage as good as this must be added to the wish life in any bedroom, his or hers!

use every day: keys, cell phone, watches, cuff links, and perhaps suspenders. These are things you take off when you get home, and they need their own home in the walk-in closet or dressing room.

HERS

Jewelry & watches	Hats
Shoes and boots	Scarves
Photographs	Ornaments

General items such as books, computers, CDs, DVDs, and video games might also be added to your list of items to store.

Also, does your young baby sleep in the room with you? If so, you will need a cupboard or a large drawer in which to keep the baby's everyday items close by.

Some people like to exercise in the privacy of their own bedroom. If you are one of these, you will need a place to store the exercise equipment.

CLOSET SYSTEMS

A well-appointed closet can feature a myriad of features to make your life easier. Whether the closet is to be custom designed or bought as a precut package, the following information might be useful.

The materials for the casings can range from particleboard with melamine or wood veneer to natural wood. Shelves and baskets can be vinyl-coated steel wire and RTA laminate. Some are epoxy-coated steel wire in white or platinum. Luxury finishes ranging from durable satin nickel and natural wood to laminate and paint offer design opportunities.

Opposite

The desirable feature here is the worktop surface on the central storage unit, handy for placing all sorts of personal items.

To discourage moths you might like to use cedar wood for some areas in the closet. A wardrobe lined in cedar is successful as a moth repellent.

One of the benefits of a room designed as a closet is the inclusion of a tabletop area that offers the chance to lay out the next day's outfit, check the contents of pockets or a briefcase, or pack a suitcase.

If you do not have a spare room, try to gain more space for a walk-in closet, or plan a large, reach-in wardrobe.

As stated in the previous pages, all of the measurements are important when planning how to make the most of space, regardless of whether it is a walk-in or a reach-in closet.

Reach-in wardrobes feature the same items as a walk-in closet, just in a smaller space. The main features to incorporate include adjustable shelving, double hanging sections, shoe bins, and a drawer unit for small accessories.

Try to provide visual access to all parts of a closet. From the outside, sliding doors might hide half of your clothes, so consider fitting bi-fold doors or frosted doors for a glimpse of what's inside.

Once the doors are open, lights placed in strategic areas make choosing which garments to wear much easier.

INSIDE DETAILS

Individual compartments within the closet frame can be designed and sized for various garments and can feature hanging rails, open shelving, drawers, and pull-out units.

HANGING RAILS

All wardrobes have one fixed hanging rail, usually set at eye level, or there can be two levels for shorter hanging garments.

Pull-down rods are useful. They feature smooth hydraulic hinges and are adjustable width-wise. An easy-access handle allows you to reach shirts and blouses hanging on a space-saving top rail.

Hanging rails can be illuminated to allow you to see your choices. Constructed in rigid aluminium and clear acrylic, the rails are powered by a low-energy fluorescent tube.

SHELVES

Shelving can be fixed or adjustable, and installed at the full height of the unit or perhaps just the top (or lower) half to allow for additional compartments.

Usually, closet shelves are constructed in plywood, solid timber, or MDF, with a veneer or a paint finish. If you prefer to air the clothing when it is stored, use shelves with a slight gap between them to allow air to pass between the shelf levels.

Some systems feature open shelving so you can slip containers onto the shelf, thus eliminating clutter. Transparent boxes for hats, gloves, and other smaller accessories are useful. Take a detailed look at the types of storage made by the major brands; visit a store or arrange for a catalog to be delivered.

Cast your eye carefully over the photographs and the accompanying details to find a style you like. Take measurements of your closet space, and of the type you like, to make sure the containers will fit into the compartments on your existing shelves.

Above

A dressing table made of translucent plastic is in the perfect location in front of a window. The natural light is excellent for a make-up session.

Right

A cream armoire in the Gustavian style is used for storing quilts and other bedding during summer months. Glass doors allow you to see at a glance what's stored on the shelves.

Left
Pre-loved furniture
can look just as
appealing in the
right location as a
new piece would.
This one has heaps
of character.

Opposite
A marble-topped
dressing table, with
a base made of
black wood, can
store much in this
bedroom alcove.

Open shelving constructed at an angle is available for shoes, and shelves above cupboards are great for storing hat boxes and other larger boxes that need a place to go.

DRAWERS
Open-fronted, glass-fronted, or closed-in drawers can conveniently store small garments such as shirts or sweaters, and accessories such as belts and ties. The idea is to be able to reach everything easily.

Check to see how easily a drawer slides on its rollers before buying. There is nothing worse than a drawer catching on its rollers every time you use it.

PULL-OUT UNITS
Pull-out features are available in just about all closet systems. They include trouser racks, tie and belt racks, a heated trouser press, and accessory trays.

Wire baskets and open containers are best for items that need to breathe, such as wool and cotton sweaters. Shoes also need to let air flow around them, and in a damp environment wire baskets are ideal, as are hanging shoe units with Velcro flaps that wrap around a hanging rail.

Pull-out trouser rails allow you to hang trousers over metal or smooth wood hangers, making it easier to select colors and styles.

Left

The open
cupboard doors
reveal a study area
with a shelf for a
computer and a
pull-out keyboard.

sealer, and change the handles. The current
desirable fashion item is a chest of drawers
constructed of mirror, sometimes with a
beveled edge and an etched border.

Buy drawer liners that add a faint
fragrance, and use a natural moth repellent if
storing precious woolens.

BEDSIDE CUPBOARDS

With drawers and doors, or both, bedside
storage is a useful area for books, personal
items, perfumed candles, magazines, the
alarm clock, and your wristwatch. Select a
style to match the bed and the decor.

TRUNKS

Often found at the bottom of a bed, the trunk,
with a lift-up lid, is a great place to store
blankets, pillows, and extra bed linen for
guests. If you live in a small apartment, a
trunk is useful for lots of things, and it can
even be used as an extra seat.

DRESSING TABLES

The dressing table is appearing in many more
modern bedrooms as women realize its
usefulness in a household where more than
one person wants to use the bathroom at the

OUT OF THE CLOSET

Other types of storage might include a free-
standing chest of drawers, bedside tables,
dressing tables, and storage trunks. Open
shelving pinned to the wall is excellent for
displaying pottery or glass art works.

CHESTS OF DRAWERS

Many styles, in different widths and heights,
are available. The best advice is to select one
that matches your décor and will be timeless.
If your existing one is just a bit faded, you
could restore it with a fresh coat of paint or

same time. Now, it's the preferred place for women to store their beauty lotions, makeup, and hair accessories.

TEEN STORAGE

Teaching teens to be organized means making it fun. Keep it colorful, creative, and individual, and the teen will be hooked on harmony. Plan how and where storage units are to go before you buy them, and look for function as well as a cool design.

Small children need small containers for crayons, stickers, and scraps they love, as well as for toys and books.

A computer table and printer ought to be placed at an ergonomically correct height, with a good chair for back support, so the teenager is comfortable while studying. A filing cabinet is handy for student papers and research books. These are now made in many bright colors in both metal and wood, with or without the addition of casters.

Above

A reach-in closet set into this child's bedroom is well organized with shelving and fabric-covered boxes.

Right

A combination of pull-out wire baskets and small compartments works well.

LIGHTING

Lighting is an exciting

element of bedroom design,

especially as the latest

technology can provide the

impetus for sweet dreams.

CONTROL LIGHT

Decorating creates a theme for a room, and lighting sets the mood. Imagine going to the theater and seeing a ballet performed under strip lights. It would not be the same as when performed under a range of different light sources that create illusions, such as a frozen lake, or a sun setting across a make-believe horizon. Your bedroom deserves to be lit properly by both daylight and artificial light.

DAYLIGHT OPTIONS

The best light to have in any bedroom when waking and getting dressed is natural light. It is better to check colors with daylight than with any other form of artificial light. However, there are a few issues you need to consider.

Bright daylight, especially sunlight, will fade clothes, and daylight is not so useful when you are trying to sleep, so controlling it is important. Depending on the time of year and your live/work routines, you may need to eliminate daylight with heavy curtains or blinds that sit close to the window.

Shutters, too, can let a controlled amount of light into a bedroom and offer extra privacy, depending on the angle at which they are set. However, shutters do not shut daylight or street lights out completely.

You can also adjust drapes to create patterns by combining them with transparent silks or foils. Not so commonly used, but not to be forgotten, is stained glass or mobiles made of colored glass and other transparent items that will refract light into the room. When a gentle wind blows, unique light patterns are created on the walls, floor, and ceiling. Nature's lighting system!

PLAN YOUR LIGHTING

Let's face it, you will probably be in the bedroom in the hours of darkness, so lighting is important if you want to create a sensual and intriguing atmosphere. Also, you will require different light for different times of the day, because the bedroom is a multipurpose room on many occasions.

Driving the plan is, of course, the budget. You can spend thousands of dollars on a dreamy lighting plan if you have both the money to spend and the opportunity to install a lighting plan from scratch.

When money is no object, you can consider the installation of a color-changing system, radio-control dimmers, perhaps a

Above
A window with a wide sill lets in natural light, while a contemporary lamp will add a light source when the daylight has gone.

Opposite
A lamp for reading and a lamp for highlighting a sculpture create two pools of light.

light sculpture, or a lighting sequence that follows the seasons of the year. These can be custom made and linked to an automated home system.

For most people, a bedroom lighting plan will not cost thousands of dollars. It could involve a central light pendant or strip of lights, bedside lamps, and uplighters to throw light around the perimeters.

It is still a good idea to get value for your money when sourcing light fittings. Even though you adore a modern fitting, you have to ask if it will remain fashionable, or go out of fashion quickly.

To start an artificial lighting plan, make a list of what you want the light to do in the bedroom. Do you want to relax, read, dress, or sleep with a light on?

Soft, seductive lighting can be created by bouncing light. A good lighting planner can determine how to use the walls, the ceilings, the floor, and the furniture to indirectly gain light for the room. By directing light sources away from the bed and toward these other surfaces you will automatically soften the light and add a calming effect.

LIGHT FOR RELAXING

This is perhaps the most common request, and one easy way to achieve an ambient mood is to direct light sources away from the bed. You could also add dimmer switches to

Left
Five colorful lamps on a stand add character
to this already bright teen's room.

lights in the room, plus use warm, colored lamps and soft-toned shades to finish the relaxing effect.

LIGHT FOR READING

The selection and placement of reading lights close to a bed requires you to consider the partner who wants to sleep in the same bed as you. Special LED (Light Emitting Diode) bulbs that give just the right amount of light are very directional, since they are built into the end of a flexible arm that moves into almost any position. Traditional bedside lamps and shades may better suit your decorating scheme, but the light they emit is definitely less directional and not the best for reading.

DRESSING & MAKEUP AREA

For dressing and makeup areas, two forms of lighting can be combined. Spotlights, spaced around the ceiling, will create pools of light that shine down. The width of the ray of light will depend on the width of the light bulbs. These pools are fine for dressing.

A direct light source is much better for bringing light onto the face when making up for the evening than an indirect source. Some modern mirrors have an integral light source designed just for this purpose.

For a more professional lighting source, try placing a series of small and low-wattage bulbs down each side of the mirror so that the lights shine directly onto your face, creating a classic Hollywood lighting effect. Be dazzled. Or, you can place a light at the top of the mirror to shine on your face.

Here are a few fitting options to consider when planning the lighting for your bedroom.

PENDANT FITTINGS

You must take care with this type of light, since it is already fitted to the center of the room. Light shining out from a central source and in all directions can flatten the bedroom's atmosphere. Often the fitting is in the wrong position, shining light behind you rather than onto you when you are dressing and checking yourself in the mirror. Perhaps replace a central pendant light with a small

Above

A strip of lights hanging from a dark ceiling will add highlights in this somber decorating scheme.

strip of spotlights, which can be directed around the room, thus creating a better ambience. Try directing one at a favorite picture, another at the wardrobe, and maybe one or two directly down to the floor area, creating pools of light. This will be a more effective plan.

However, if you want to just change the shade, buy one that reflects the theme, and do not be afraid to cut down on the amount of light emitting from it.

UPLIGHTING

This is a great way to add mood to a room. By careful positioning of uplights you can brighten the corners of a room, or you can place them behind plants or furniture to add a new dynamic to any space. This is an amazing way to make a theatrical effect.

LOW-ENERGY LIGHTING

The most misunderstood, environmentally friendly method of bringing light into a room, low-energy lighting is much easier on your pocketbook in the medium to long term. The bulbs seems to have been tagged with an unfashionable label, which is a shame.

Fluorescent tubes and the newer compact fluorescent lamps (CFLs) come into this low-energy category, and are underused in a bedroom. These lamps can last 12 times longer than conventional lamps. The older fluorescent tubes gave out a cold light. Now, a range of colored sleeves is available for fluorescent tubes, which give off hues of whatever color you choose.

In bedrooms where light is a problem, and you need to have the light on for longer than usual, fluorescents are inexpensive both to buy and to run.

They are great for ambient lighting, especially when used as uplighting above a pelmet. They are also used in many storage systems, such as in a closet to throw light into the darker areas.

The appearance of any light source can be changed by the use of a filter, such as those used in photographic studios when a change of mood is required. Any transparent fire-safe material can be placed over a low-energy light fitting, as long as it does not directly touch the bulb. Preferably, the filter ought to be on a frame or a good few inches (centimeters) away from the light bulb. Low energy bulbs have low heat output; however, you must be very careful not to create a fire risk. You can try interesting crinkly paper set over a wire frame or a fireproof fabric, also pulled tight over a wire frame, for effect.

Whatever type of filter you use, please use caution.

CANDLES

A burning candle does present a fire risk but there are many lovely glass and ceramic candleholders that make burning votive candles much safer than in the past.

You can burn scented candles in the bedroom in much the same way as you burn them in the bathroom. Candlelight is romantic and relaxing. It is an excellent idea to keep a small pitcher of water handy just in case something untoward does happen!

LED AND FIBER OPTICS

A plethora of technically advanced light sources is now available, and each is capable of creating a unique light effect. LED lights are manufactured in varying colors and sizes, and use very little energy. In fact, some use so little energy that you could leave them on throughout the night as safety lighting. Most of the LED fittings have a low light output so they make excellent night-lights.

LED lights are now also being produced in RGB (Red, Green, Blue), and by mixing them together in differing ways you can create anything from a white light to any color in the rainbow. If pink is your passion, then the light can be pink for a determined time; when your mood turns, so can the color: to blue, violet, amber, yellow, green, or red; or it can be set to a continuous color-changing mode from sunrise to sunset. If you think you would like to implement this type of effect, consult a lighting expert before installing a kit.

There are many sites on the Internet to help you make up your mind as to the type of LED effect you want.

Fiber optics use a single light source to travel through fibers to an end source. Use tiny fiber optics to set a unique Milky Way of stars in the ceiling. With an added color wheel, each star can slowly pass through a series of colors or go on and off at differing times and appear to twinkle.

Low-output laser lights can create amazing moving patterns across the ceiling and around the room.

However, for most of us the concept of lighting for a bedroom is quite simple. We do not necessarily need special effects or color-changing lights to create the bedroom of our dreams. That said, all of us can benefit from a litle knowledge of how lighting works and a design direction. As the cost of a dramatic light-changing system is lowered, you just might be tempted to install one, though.

Above

A classic translucent lamp base sits beside a silver tray, and is topped with a simple shade in keeping with the elegant lines of the bedroom.

PART TWO

CASE STUDIES

Set on a corner block in a lush setting, this sleek master bedroom is in the home of a busy young architect and his family.

MODERNIST IN SUBURBIA

The first impression you get when walking into this light and airy bedroom is that you have arrived in a place where "minimal" means minimal. The design is pared back to the essentials, leaving the textures of the flooring, curtains, and bedcover to shine.

You are then drawn to the large, sliding glass doors that open up on either side of the room. Slip through the silk billowing in the breeze onto a large, open deck area and you immediately understand why the 37-year-old architect David Thompson and his family chose this location to live.

On the not-too-far horizon are the Santa Monica mountains; at sunset this is where you will find the architect, his wife, and their young daughter, plus anyone lucky enough to be invited for early evening drinks. "The sunset is tremendous from here," says David, with the look of a man enchanted.

This is a house designed for the California lifestyle; it is indoor/outdoor living personified.

Above
A fluffy, natural sheepskin rug offers warmth to the feet.

Opposite
Dark wood is a contrast to the painted walls behind the bed.

The exterior of the home is made from cedar, with large picture windows. On the bedroom level, the flooring is an expanse of bamboo, a decision made not only because they like the color of its finish but also because it is an ecologically sound design decision.

The aluminum-framed, large glass sliding doors are a major feature here, too. The industrial nature of the doors gives a store-front feel; when you roll them back into place after a day in the open air, it is as if you are shutting up shop for the night, safely enclosing the room and its occupants. A strong corner pole, which helps support the roof in each corner of the room, is the meeting point for the sliding doors when closed.

Covering the glass expanse with fabric for privacy was an interesting challenge, solved in

Top left
A combination of patterns and colors adds a light touch to the expanse of the green bedcover.

Left
Sited for comfortable bedtime viewing is this flatscreen television, also wired to the home's audio system.

stages. Initially, a floor-length set of curtains in a chocolate brown Knoll fabric with a black-out lining was installed on a curtain track attached to the ceiling. After a few weeks the couple felt something else was needed to complete the effect, so a shimmery silk fabric in a light green color was added as an outer layer.

Now, when the doors are open and the curtains are pulled across to form a wall of curtains, the fabrics and the breeze combined add an unexpected dimension to the bedroom. It is as if the owners ordered a series of small performances by nature and had box seats to the event. As flames in a fireplace are slightly hypnotic, so is the billowing of the silk fabric; time and time again, you watch for its gentle movement, admiring its eloquent elegance. "I like the ephemeral quality of the billowing effect against the rectilinear lines," says the architect in David.

And so to the bed. The story goes that the couple were staying in a hotel in Big Sur, California, and liked the bed so much they ordered one for their new home. They stayed in a lot of hotels, testing out the beds, before deciding on this one from the Post Ranch Inn. The mattress is a box spring design, and the dark wood bed surround is meant to look like a platform bed. It does. The bed is placed at the same orientation as the deck outside.

A stylish architectural feature goes almost unnoticed, until you look at the walls more closely. The floor and walls meet seamlessly; the absence of a wood skirting board is a fine detail adding to the clean lines in the entire master bedroom and its ensuite bath. This same detail continues throughout the home.

At first glance, again, the forms of the dark furniture and the bed surround seem edgy, yet they are balanced by the softness of the textural surfaces inherent in the fabrics used

for the curtains and the bedcover. On the tall, wood-framed bed head a pale, aqua-gray fabric has a nobbly texture, offering comfort to heads when watching television or DVDs on the flatscreen television located on the wall opposite the end of the bed. There was a long debate about whether or not they ought to have a television in the bedroom. As their daughter grows up, they figure she will want to watch movies with friends, and what better place to watch them than in the bedroom, while the adults entertain downstairs.

"We watch movies here, too," he adds, admitting he is a bit of a gadget goofball: the house is wired for music in every room.

Above

A place for shoes, bags, accessories, and clothes is located behind the bedroom, in a wide corridor that leads to the bathroom.

The couple "kind of fell into" the color scheme. There is a definite family of colors in natural materials working together in the bedroom, selected to bring out the richness of the exotic wood seen in the chest of drawers, bedside tables and storage unit (placed under the television screen).

The dark, rich walnut cabinetry is David's own design, sleek and discreet, and yet practical. The top of the chest of drawers doubles as a place to put coffee-table books; the television storage unit is topped with a sheet of toughened glass.

The wood helps to merge the inside with the outside, since the deck is constructed in a Brazilian hardwood with a natural oil finish for its own protection. A vinyl rug adds color, and a corner unit manufactured of plastic wicker is made more comfortable with soft, outdoor cushions covered in a cream fabric. David has visions of a hammock out here on the deck, for lounging, and a sun umbrella for shade, as well as more of the same furniture.

Back inside, the bamboo floor leads through to a walk-through dressing room, where there is a space for shoes, clothes, accessories, and photographs. It is a neat design, in keeping with the order elsewhere in the bedroom.

This master suite is an example of a planned living space; it is a bedroom that will not be used for sleep only, but as a place for family. All of the design elements are firmly in place for this home to grow, at ease with itself within the parameters set by the architect.

DESIGN SUMMARY

▶ Custom-designed furniture made in rich walnut

▶ Flooring throughout is bamboo

▶ Sliding doors on industrial rollers disappear into walls

▶ Wood floor in the hall area

Above
When the breeze blows, the metallic curtain wafts onto the deck.

Opposite
The deck seen from the master bedroom.

FIT FOR A PRINCESS

enchanting about the room is the reflection of the landscape outside. A window and an aluminum-framed glass door that slides along rollers (as in the parents' room) serve to bring foliage from surrounding trees into the room. Colored parrots live in nearby trees and flit pass every now and then, adding to the feeling you are somewhere exotic. The combination of cream, green, live parrots, and painted animals creates an imaginative impression of a very pleasant jungle walk.

The crib for the young daughter who inhabits this bedroom is well positioned so she can talk to the animals before falling asleep. When she is a little older, the crib will be replaced by a bed.

Color plays the major role in the decoration here. Pink, turquoise, green, and red dominate in accessories, while the cream walls provide the perfect backdrop for the mountain. Everything else has been kept simple, including the bamboo flooring which flows from the master bedroom across the hall and into their daughter's room. A comfortable nursing chair, a chest of drawers, and a small child-sized table in the middle of the room, where the daughter and her friends draw, are the only other pieces of furniture.

Along one wall, though, is another surprise. There is a child's kitchen, complete with an oven, a stove top, a sink and faucet, and cupboards. Bought as a kit, her grandfather put it together. It suits the room

Across the hall from the master bedroom is daughter Lily's room, which is a colorful delight. But wait! What's that walking across the wall? An elephant, followed closely by a pig, a monkey, a duck, a kangaroo, a hippo, and a hungry-looking giraffe.

They're walking along a mountain ridge, the slope of which is painted on the wall in a block of green. They've stopped in front of a little girl, to take a breath before marching on. This captivating animal mural was painted by David's father, also an architect. What is so

Left
The sliding door leads to the deck, which looks over trees to the right.

Opposite
The animals walk in single file atop the mountain ridge, enjoying the view of the colorful room.

and is painted in paler hues of the other colors seen in the rug and the storage boxes lined up along the foothills of the green mountain wall. A rug in colors that match these soft-to-touch boxes was found by chance and now looks as if it was custom made.

Behind the mountain wall is a private bathroom where a zebra waits by the bath for bath-time conversations.

The room features a ceiling fan and air conditioning for days when the temperature is too hot or too cold, when the door is pulled across, enclosing the room. The drapes in this little girl's room are the same triple thickness of the chocolate brown fabric, black-out lining, and green silk used in the master bedroom, providing visual continuity when you look at the house from the street outside.

To grow up surrounded by clean lines, vibrant colors, and natural materials might encourage this child to appreciate the worth of architectural design and to enjoy the pleasure that good use of space can bring.

Top
This child's kitchen, made from a kit, is a major feature in the bedroom.

Above
Bold colors in both the rug on the floor and the storage boxes make for a cheerful atmosphere.

DESIGN SUMMARY

▶ Flooring made from bamboo

▶ Wall surfaces painted in two tones, cream and green

▶ Bedroom opens to a small deck, providing indoor/outdoor living

▶ Curtains same as in master suite

▶ Central ceiling fan provides cool air

BEACHSIDE
SERENITY

Designer Wendy Richens and her
California client have a long history
together. Their working relationship
began when Wendy was hired to
design and decorate the client's first
residence back in 1987.

As it happens, this is the second time she has decorated the master bedroom suite in his current home. The first time Wendy worked on the bedroom was four years ago.

Then, he was single and the room had a masculine feel with heavy roman shades, white walls, and halogen lighting. Now that he is married with a child, Wendy has transformed the bachelor bedroom to a comfortable master suite better suited for a family man.

Situated at one end of the 7,000-square-foot (278.8 square meter) hilltop residence, the large master bedroom suite is secluded from the rest of the home, and is reached via double doors and a long, discreetly lit hallway that lead into the main sleeping area, creating an aura of privacy.

The suite was gutted to reconfigure the space to make it more efficient. Since the area would now be shared, adding more storage was a priority. Large his-and-hers walk-in closets now line the entrance hall to organize clothing and other belongings out of sight of the bedroom. With the utilitarian aspect contained in the hallway, the result is a sleeping area utterly devoted to luxury.

Wendy's attention to detail defines the stately nature of the master bedroom. Lining the long hallway, a series of stone ledges set against wood panels and repeated squared arches make a passageway that establishes the mood and sets the stylish tone. Brazilian hardwood flooring and reverse-cut baseboards recessed into the drywall add to the silhouette.

Opposite
The impressive bed
was custom
designed by
Wendy Richens.

Above
The three figures
seem to stand as
protectors at the
bottom of the bed
in the master suite.

Left

A cream shade blends with the pale green silk fabric drapes behind.

Opposite

Textured pillow covers add more comfort to the bed.

Overleaf

The view along the long hall leading to the bedroom suite, and the fireplace and the fish tank located opposite the bed, built into an exterior wall.

Inside the sleeping area, a silk-draped window wall that runs along one side of the room adds privacy that shields the room from the morning sun. The pale green fabric gives the room a sophisticated lift. Remote control units on the curtain panels make it possible to operate the draperies from anywhere in the room.

Buttery, cream walls elsewhere in the suite complement the window panels and add a layer of color that warms up the space. A mahogany bed anchors the sleeping area. The picture frame-style headboard features padded leather panels, saddle stitched and set into wood trim dividers. Nestled at the foot of the bed is a custom-built pop-up television cabinet; a mechanized lid that lifts to reveal a state-of-the-art television.

Across the room, a limestone fireplace sits at the center of a seating area appointed with luxuriously soft chenille-covered armchairs. Next to the fireplace, a freshwater fish tank built into a recessed cabinet creates a tranquil scene. The cabinet is reinforced to take the weight of the tank. Storage is underneath.

The art collection stands out as the one feature that personalizes the suite. Here, Wendy integrated an eclectic collection of statuary, masks, swords, and paintings bought around the world. The key is the lighting plan. The designer replaced the room's halogen lights with incandescent pinpoint fixtures that highlight the collection. Connected to a single switch, the effect of the pinpoints is breathtaking as the rest of the room falls away and the collection takes center stage in the elegant master suite.

DESIGN SUMMARY

▶ Main wall surfaces painted a butter cream color

▶ Impressive television cabinet designed by Wendy Richens

▶ Furnishings are soft for comfort throughout the suite

▶ Wood floor in hall area

Clean lines, reflective surfaces, and an eclectic mix of furniture styles combine in this master bedroom, and as a result, it shines.

A CASE OF UNCLUTTERED EXPRESSION

Designer Marisa Solomon and architect John Reed's hilltop home in California represents a quintessential meeting of the minds. John's architectural projects reflect his modernist approach: clean, linear, and contemporary. Marisa, on the other hand, has a deep admiration for John's work but approaches design from a more traditional point of view. Collaborating is nothing new to the couple, who have worked in tandem on design projects for a broad range of clients. However,

this, their own home, was their first foray into building and designing a space they would ultimately live in together.

The product is a stunning, contemporary dwelling set high on a hill with breathtaking views of the surrounding valley and city lights in the distance.

Within the framework of the structure, Marisa and John crafted a master bedroom suite that stands out not only as one of the home's architectural highlights, but also as a

Opposite

The color scheme is black and white with a touch of artichoke green hue on the smooth walls.

Above

An antique wood and mirror panel reflects the room's beauty

Opposite

The key to this comfort zone is in the soft
edges of the furniture and the view.

Above

A fabulous dressing table with smooth
rounded edges is located in an alcove.

DESIGN SUMMARY

► Decorating scheme is a combination
of modern and traditional styles

► All cabinetry is black for impact

► Chandelier light is supplemented by
discreet downlights set in the ceiling
retreat mood

► Natural light dominates during the day

► Black floorboards have reflective
qualities

noteworthy example of the melding of two
design sensibilities, with spectacular results.

"It worked well. I never questioned John
on the architecture of the home and he never
questioned me on the design," says Marisa.
Consequently there isn't one predominant
style. Both contemporary and traditional
elements were used in a balanced way.

With five children between them, the large
bedroom suite is designed as a refuge from
what can be at times a bustling household.
"It's a place where the two of us can go to
close the door and turn off the rest of the
world," Marisa explains.

Accessed through a private corridor, the
master suite is made up of the bedroom,
dressing area, and spa bath. It occupies one
end of the large home. Here, John took
advantage of the property's privacy and views
to design an open, loft-like setting with a
sweeping, L-shaped window wall that wraps
around the large bedroom and creates its most
dramatic focal point.

While the expanse of glass and the
amount of light would typically represent
contemporary detailing, wood mullions tone
down the effect of the windows, introducing a
more traditional feel without diminishing their
impact. Overhead, a barrel ceiling adds subtle
architectural interest that similarly softens the
lines of the large room.

The appealing color palette, a mélange of
artichoke green walls, crisp white trim, and
deep espresso brown wood flooring, provides
a framework for custom furnishings.

The furniture is contemporary but with
classic lines. On the bed, a dark wood frame
with square corners is softened with suede
fabric inserts that match the wall color. Layers
of white linen, silk, and organza line the bed.

Above

The room with a view by day . . .

Across from the bed and next to the windows, Marisa placed a pair of upholstered silk chaise lounges where the couple enjoy a quiet moment to relax and take in the panoramic views from the picture windows. On an adjacent wall, a plasma television mounted on a swivel arm extends for viewing from various angles throughout the room.

In addition to the room's well-executed form and its simply chic furnishings, it is Marisa's connection to history, as well as a lifelong passion for collecting beautiful objects, that gives the room its true personality.

Marisa believes accessories and objects that carry meaning are what give a room its warmth. Indeed, a personal collection of silver

candlesticks, crystal perfume bottles, and an antique chandelier present a connection to the past that stands in contrast to the bedroom's contemporary style. Against one wall, a stunning 17th-century architectural ornate panel, incorporating a mirror and oil canvas within its carved frame, visually bridges the gap between modern and traditional design. To

Marisa, historic pieces are a reminder of where where everything started. "John's passion for architecture began with a visit to Italy when he was fourteen. He went on to define his own style, but it began with ancient Roman architecture." Collaboration with John on projects has resulted in a shift in her own design trajectory: she likes modern style.

Above

. . . and by night. Serenity is the overwhelming mood in both scenarios.

HIS & HERS

For a young couple just starting out, decorating a new home can create any number of design dilemmas.

Above

Soft tones and smooth finished fabrics are used for pillow covers and the bedcover.

Right

A magnificent, modern four-poster bed sits in a light-filled room with grand proportions.

For example, he lives for the latest technology; she could take it or leave it. She may dream of a six-burner professional range in the kitchen, while he is just as happy with takeout. In the end, it is the fine balance between the needs and wants of both the husband and the wife that transforms an ordinary house into a home.

Perhaps nowhere is this balance between the two more important than when it comes to decorating the master bedroom. For designer Joani Stewart of Santa Monica's Montana Avenue Interiors, the challenge came in the form of a stunning, four-story home in Marina Del Rey, California, purchased by the couple.

"It was their first home," says Joani. "We wanted to create a master bedroom that was comfortable, casual, and very personal; a space where they could relax and enjoy spending time together."

From the start of the project, the couple made decisions together to determine the direction of the room.

The result of the collaboration is a bedroom that delicately balances both sensibilities in appearing neither too masculine, nor too feminine. To accomplish this goal, the designer paired repeated geometric shapes that lend substance with sumptuous bedding, draperies, and upholstery to soften the feel of the retreat.

An impressive four-poster bed, the couple's first furniture find, anchors the sleeping area with sculptural lines. On either side of the bed, nightstands offer storage along with display space for mementos.

An upholstered bench at the foot of the bed balances the large piece of furniture and adds a practical place to sit while putting on shoes. "Every bedroom needs that," she says.

The heart of the room is a comfortable seating area, perfectly proportioned to fit the long, rectangular-shaped space. Arranged in front of a fireplace and large, plasma screen TV, the area includes a plush sofa, two ultrasuede chairs and a clever, Italian leather coffee table with cushions that convert to serving trays for cocktails or a dinner for two.

Tall transom windows and glass French doors bask the room with natural light—an appealing attribute during most of the day, but a bit of a bother on sunny weekend mornings. Here, Joani remedied the situation with window coverings that alternately filter and block light from the room. On the windows, linen Roman shades diffuse and filter the sun's rays while allowing light to flow into the room. To fully block the light, luxurious drapery panels inter-lined with blackout fabric pull across the French doors to protect furnishings and fabrics and ensure a sound slumber. Elsewhere, plush bed linens, soft pillows, and luxurious throws create cuddle-down comfort that counterbalances the geometric lines of the room and its furnishings.

Opposite
The room as seen from the bed, taking in the fireplace, the flat-screen television and a seating area.

Below
Soft, suede finish upholstery beckons.

Above

A clever small occasional table
constructed of leather includes a
wood tray as a practical feature.

DESIGN SUMMARY

▶ Main wall surfaces painted a calm neutral shade

▶ Soft furnishings are smooth and soft in texture

▶ Colors all muted to create a calm retreat mood

▶ Natural light dominates

▶ Floor surfaces covered with plush pile carpet

▶ Fireplace set into wall below flat-screen television makes room airy

Above and Left

Fabric plays a major role in providing the comfort in this seating area, making the bedroom comfortable and contemporary without being sleek.

The journey through the house to this bedroom takes you through a traditional Arts & Crafts style home in a suburb of San Francisco.

When you open the door to this bedroom and step inside you are taken into another realm. The double-height room is breathtaking on first acquaintance. It is such a delight of pure architectural play that it is only when you begin to examine the parts of the entirety that you realize its design has been executed with almost military precision. Every individual detail has been conceived to be in harmony with the master plan for this master bedroom and its ensuite.

Above
Designed for reading, this black lamp is the perfect bedtime companion.

Opposite
A painting from the *Bush Medicine* series by Aboriginal artist Gloria Petyarre of the Anmatyerre people.

HOME AS A REFUGE

From the woven bed
frame to the suede
fabric drapes, the
design story is based
on texture.

"We changed the map of the bedroom floor,"
explains Nestor Matthews, the architect. "We
popped the ceiling up and added four small
windows in the elevated ceiling section, which
made the room much larger".

The clients had seen a bathroom Nestor
had done for another client and approached
him to redesign their kitchen. How the tower
was conceived is another story. Nestor saw
the kitchen remodel as an opportunity to
create a tower that would add an impressive

dimension to the existing house. He envisaged
a dramatic space, which in practical terms also
enabled him to site a master bath adjacent to
the new master bedroom, set above the new
kitchen. (This was a home with three bedrooms
and only one bathroom prior to the redesign.)

The architect and the clients negotiated
the usual pitfalls that are inherent in a
collaboration to happily discover they had
similar concepts in mind. A lot of discussion
back and forth between architect and client

covered all the potential design opportunities, with the final plan gaining approval from all sides. The influences of both the architect and his particular clients are on display in the master bedroom. The clients were brave and sneaked in a few of their favorite things when the architect wasn't looking, such as the leather chair, seen and desired by the husband, so he brought it into the scheme.

In each corner of the bedroom are small square "lookouts" to emphasise the tower concept. In a bygone era, these would have been an essential part of a fortress tower's construction. Now these are merely decorative, adding glorious light into the room. The wood window frames are painted in keeping with the design brief to keep everything light.

The home is from the Arts & Crafts period, a classic, solid house with its own character and definite style. The addition of the tower has been a seamless exercise; it blends in and feels as if it has always been on the site. The project was successful in creating an openness and feeling of lightness in a house which traditionally has formal dark wood on the ground floor.

The clients were simultaneously working on a master plan for the garden, which can be seen from the new master bedroom. As the plants and shrubs in the redesigned garden grew into maturity, the owners were treated to a display of fresh verdant foliage and flowers from the bedroom windows. It proved successful in bringing the outside inside the redesigned bedroom.

One of the benefits of the renewed bedroom is the proximity of the ensuite. The entrance to it is via a sliding door located at the bed head end of the room, which leads to a short passage. The walk-in closet is behind closed doors to the right. In the walk-in closet,

Top
Giving the impression of lookouts from a tower, these windows let in more light to the spacious room.

Above
Suede fabric stamped with small holes becomes a kaleidoscope when the sunlight pours through, making patterns around the walls.

DESIGN SUMMARY

▶ Main wall and floor surfaces painted
  in harmonious pale colors

▶ Pod cabinetry for the television
  custom made by Nestor Matthews

▶ Chocolate-colored wicker bed frame
  makes strong statement in space

▶ Natural light dominates

▶ Neutral textured cream carpet provides
  discreet foundation for bedroom

there is a clever, custom-made, three-panel mirror that enables you to see the front, back, and sides of yourself before you leave.

A new, wool sisal carpet with a subtle check pattern, called Zanzibar in Bamboo color, covers the floor. The paintwork is in two shades: on the walls is Benjamin Moore's color 904, and the trim and ceiling above the bed are in HC45.

"We liked Nestor's simplicity and understated elegance," remarks the client. The trio were also in agreement with the color spectrum: neutrals and taupe dominate the decorating scheme. "We like light colors," they say agreeably.

The architect convinced his clients to replace the waterbed with a new bed that features a strong, chocolate wicker frame.

Nestor designed the original steel and rubber chest of drawers. It has a brushed stainless steel top and black rubber on the front of the drawers. Hanging above the drawers is an intriguing embroidered fabric piece set in a wood frame. Its subtle design was woven in Indonesia and the piece was brought back by the client, carefully wrapped, in her luggage. The tan leather chair with a chocolate brown back was discovered by the clients and added to the scheme. It provides a place to read a book and has a small ceramic table by its side.

Nestor also designed the cream-colored pod cabinet on wheels to house a television and a DVD player, plus storage shelves. Manufactured from particleboard, it has a pale cream lacquer finish on the outside, with a black matte finish interior. Woven linen fabric lines the glass-fronted doors of a freestanding wardrobe unit whose frame is made from ebonized wood. Here, the couple's collection of sweaters is stored.

The curtain fabric, in a design called Elepunto by Bergamo Inc., was chosen by the husband, and is made from fine stamped felt through which sunlight produces diamante sparkles as it shines through the tiny holes in the fabric. A blind fits into the window frames sited either side of the bed head, while the drapes that hang from an iron pole can be pulled across the two larger windows.

Above the bed is a painting from the *Bush Medicine* series by Aboriginal artist Gloria Petyarre of the Anmatyerre people from the settlement of Utopia in Australia.

Above

Wood, leather, and steel surfaces are softened by the presence of the Indian woven fabric hanging on the wall above the set of drawers.

When an architect is asked to create a calm environment in an existing bedroom, decorating choices can prove more challenging than when starting with a newly built space.

CROWNING GLORY

Above
Here, the small table lamp is the perfect foil to the wood texture. The shade has a trim in a color to match the linen behind.

Opposite
The padded linen headboard and its bleached white oak wings give a feeling of security. The bed linen is in a hue similar to the pale gray silk drapes.

This did not prevent the San Francisco-based architect Nestor Matthews from taking a completely new look at a room with little architectural glamour to act as a cornerstone.

His client, a successful woman, enjoyed the advantage of a small courtyard garden outside the bedroom windows, which provided a percentage of green serenity. When Nestor first saw the bedroom, he saw a colorless bed with a bright painting above it. The client did not want to deviate from a calm environment story, so Matthews concentrated on creating a comfort-filled room, using warm, soothing colors and textural interest.

Matthews looked at the choices. The issue
was how to walk in and then how to approach
the bed. "People usually like to face the door,
be in the command position. Typically, they
want to come in and see the big picture," he
says authoritatively.

The bed in question is from the bed
manufacturer McCroskey, highly rated by the
Matthews practice. It is made from natural
materials with hand-tied springs.

"The way we design is always with calmness
and serenity in mind. The challenge here was
to make the room's style and its furnishings
soft and feminine. Our designs are perhaps
perceived to be more on the masculine side,
but this client had an aesthetic that was similar
to ours," says Nestor.

To begin the makeover, he persuaded his
client to add a new floor covering throughout,
a pure wool sisal carpet in Pebblestone color.

It was selected for its textural interest and its neat, tailored look. Once this was down, the design became firm.

The next step was to look at the lighting, to create a sensual mood. The ceilings feature small recessed downlighters above the cabinetry to the left of the doorway, and a single spotlight above the bed. Stone-colored lamps sit on bedside tables by B & B Italia, which have a finish similar to the side wings.

The focal point in the room is the padded headboard which wraps around the head of the bed. Four vertical panels, covered in cream linen, are at the bed head, with a bleached, white oak panel attached to each end acting as a wing. Nestor also added a traditional touch with a handmade, fluted crown molding that travels around the top of the room. The fluted pieces were carved separately then glued side by side between two strips of molding, then sanded, finished, and painted.

All of the wood throughout the bedroom and the remainder of the apartment is bleached white oak. The feature storage unit seen at the end of the bed is a masterpiece of white oak cabinetry and displays books, sculptures, and a large ceramic plate in the section designed for a television. A full-height, narrow mirror panel to each side of the cabinet is placed to reflect light from the garden by day and the subtle lighting by night.

The cream color scheme has a subtle color addition in the form of the drapes, made of a gray silk fabric. There is also a natural woven blind at the window sill.

The simplicity of the color scheme and the texture achieve the client's wish for a feminine, sophisticated bedroom.

RETRO
MASTERPIECE

The unmistakable 1950s style of
Michael Giamio's house was
inspired by a meeting with the
original owner of his home, whom
he describes as a real modernist.

A few years after moving in, Giamio went to
visit the home's first owner, a woman now in
her nineties. Her new home was decorated in
the same mid-century style she had always
used, and it gave Michael an idea.

When he saw how she still lived and her
sense of aesthetics, he set about his own
interpretation of mid-century living. Although
Michael is not an interior designer by trade (he
works as an art director in animation) he took
on the entire redesign of his home.

Michael based his color choices on the
first owner's scheme, traces of which were still
visible in his house, and which she had used
again in her new home. They are very muddy
gold, greens, tans, and yellow-greens, colors
he realized were those you can live with
forever because they never go out of style. Two
of the walls were painted in a color called

Opposite
The Cubic light fitting is used twice in the bedroom,
on opposite walls, and elsewhere in the house to
create a link between the rooms.

Above
The additional advantage of the Formica shelves is
that they don't nick or dent, so they are more
practical for a frequently changed display.

Above

The wall that is now covered in walnut was once concealed by closets. The black-and-white photograph of Michael's mother, reframed in a simple modern frame, adds a touch of glamour.

Mellowed Ivory, which comes across as a gold-green shade.

One wall in the bedroom, leading out to the pool, is almost entirely glass. For the fourth wall, Michael had something much bolder in mind. He covered it entirely with walnut.

The shelves placed in the center of the walnut wall are made of bright yellow Formica, an unexpected combination that, again, was inspired by the former owner. "It's not something I would have thought of doing myself, to use a very expensive and a very cheap material together," Michael admits.

In the 1950s in California it was very common to have wall-to-wall carpet throughout the home, so the bedroom carpet was a suitably authentic choice. However, this was not the only reason Michael chose it.

"I do have hardwood elsewhere in the house," he says, "but I like carpet in the bedroom, especially first thing in the morning! I chose a pure wool that's variegated between golden tan and black threads."

Above

Even the smallest artifacts in the room have been chosen to fit the theme, including this 1940s carved wood bull.

The furniture was purchased from a variety of vintage stores, including Fat Chance and Futurama, which are two well-known sources for Retro-style furniture located in Los Angeles.

A lot of the furniture was refurbished. The headboard and side tables for the double bed proved to be unusually low, so Michael had to have the bed frame made specially to fit. Even the box springs were designed to be less deep than they would usually be.

Above

The bedside lamp is Scandinavian, and had to be converted by Michael's electrician before use.

Some modern furnishing items were then carefully selected to fit in with the Retro look, such as the intriguing dumbbell-shaped wall-light. Michael looked in many places for just the right streamlined light but most of them seemed, to him, a bit overblown. This Cubic light was the most subtle style he could find. Another touch was the mobile in the corner, made by Flensted Mobiles in Denmark. The plant container in a corner of the room is by an artist called David Cressey, and fits perfectly.

To cover the windows and glass door in the evenings, Michael chose vertical blinds rather than the more conventional horizontal kind. The choice was largely practical because he felt horizontal blinds to be more cumbersome to pull up and down, and in a house with a lot of windows, vertical blinds were easier and quicker to operate. They also disappear into the wall when drawn aside, and therefore they are more unobtrusive.

"I used fabric on one side rather than the usual plastic, so that they didn't look too much like office blinds," Michael says.

The paintings over the bed and on the Formica shelves reflect Michael's job as well as his love of Retro style. The works are by Mary Blair, a famous artist at the Disney Studios, who was known for being a terrific colorist. The paintings depict scenes from *Cinderella* and *Peter Pan* and add a playful element to an otherwise grown-up room.

In the quest for an authentic look, every detail was attended to, right down to the door handles, which Michael found at Liz's Antique Hardware. The design is called Luna, and the handles were manufactured by Schlage and are vintage mid-century style. They were fresh out of the box, never used.

The finishing touches were the bolsters and bedcover, which Michael designed. He chose the fabric from a place called Diamond Foam and Fabric and had it made up by a seamstress. He chose colors on the warm side of the palette, which make the room inviting.

The small chair, which Michael thinks is a Hans Wegner piece, was already covered in just the right vintage fabric, and fitted perfectly with his existing color and texture theme.

A lounger chair was reupholstered in a white bouclé material from Germany.

Now that it is completed, what appeals to Michael most about his homage to the 1950s is its charismatic warmth.

"The rest of the house has a varied roofline, with all the rooms at different heights, and this is the lowest room," he explains.

"So when you come in, it's like going into a cave. It feels warm and embracing," Michael says contentedly.

DESIGN SUMMARY

▶ Feature wall surface made of dark walnut panels

▶ Retro look was researched in great detail

▶ Authentic 1950s light fittings

Above

Natural light flooding in from the yard ensures that the room, with its dark wood wall and rich colors, is cozy rather than dark and gloomy.

THE MAN WITH THE GOLDEN TOUCH

The work of interior designer Renzo Mongiardino

was the inspiration for this texturally rich bedroom.

The owner, interior designer David Desmond, wanted to explore wall surfaces, patterns, and layers. "Renzo Mongiardino was the master of illusion and had a true understanding of how to make a room's architecture and decoration work in harmony."

For the spectacular wall treatment, David drew on Mongiardino's silver room that he saw in his mentor's book, *Roomscapes*. He thought he would try a gold room.

First, David lacquered the walls a dark brown color, using wood stain over the latex paint that was already on the walls. Using a product called Dutch Metal Leaf, which is like gold leaf but is not made of gold, he applied sizing (thin wallpaper glue) to the walls, then positioned each sheet by hand. When the sheets were dry, he rubbed the walls with balls of 00 steel wool to reveal some of the brown stain through the gold, then applied a clear matte sealer coat over the walls.

He then added a brown fabric trim all the way around the borders, "as if I had upholstered the walls in fabric and used the fabric trim to cover the tacks."

Opposite
The gold leaf sheets make a gloriously rich pattern on the walls.

Above
The red fringed shade is the perfect contrast to gold and black.

Above

The headboard
matches the
drapes and sets a
floral tone for the
bed linen.

DESIGN SUMMARY

▶ Wall surface created with brown paint
and sheets of gold leaf

▶ Colefax & Fowler floral curtains bought
on ebay auction site

▶ Dark red color accent against
gold and dark brown background

▶ Herringbone sisal floor covering

David also created a marble effect on the
baseboards by applying different colors of
wood stain over the latex paint and using a red
magic marker to add a few veins.

The room's décor developed in stages.
After the walls, the room felt unbalanced, so he
then found the curtains. To find interesting
curtains to hang alongside the stunning gold
textured wall was a big challenge. His tenacity
was rewarded when David saw a pair on ebay,
the online auction house.

"I flipped because I liked the pattern
(Colefax & Fowler's Tree Poppy) and the
swagged valance with the bullion fringe. The
curtains were in London. I won the auction,
paid online, and a box the size of a washing
machine arrived less than a week later.

"The seller did a fine job of packing,
including using talcum powder to prevent the
curtains from getting a musty smell during the
journey. I should add that the curtains were for
one 10-foot-long (approximately three-meter
long) window.

"My seamstress cut them down to fit the
two windows in the bedroom and added the
fringe to the leading edge and base. There
was just enough fabric to do my two windows.
It was really close," he says.

It was a worthwhile risk because the
curtains are perfect in their new theatrical
location. Anything less would have paled into
insignificance.

David likes the way old paint looks and
has never touched the paint on the ceiling,
cornice, door casings, and doors in eleven
years. In complete contrast to the textured
walls and patterned curtains, the floor covering
is a large herringbone-pattern sisal. There is a
short story behind the deep red bedcover. It
was found at Le Jardin Moghol during a trip to
Paris, and completes the room.

A large desk takes up the area by the large windows. Its structure is light, and it seems to float in the space, not dominate it. "I used to have a daybed there, but work has supplanted leisure. I work at night a lot, and the desk provides a spot to spread everything out."

Now that the scheme is complete, the designer is pleased with the atmosphere.

He continues to add accessories, such as the turquoise and gold eye pendant a cousin in Istanbul sent him to ward off the evil eye. It hangs from a convenient mirror.

The room can take a lot of pattern and not feel overloaded. "It is a room that wants more, more, more. And it is fun to be in, especially at night. It glows," says David Desmond.

Above

David won the ebay auction for these sumptuously patterned drapes. The chair is covered in the same fabric.

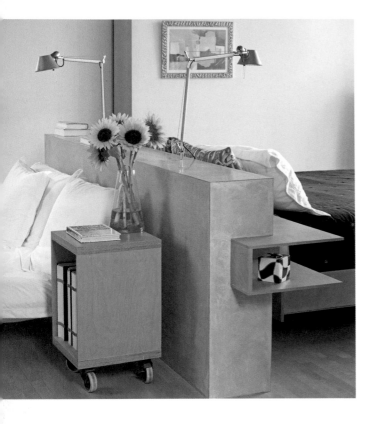

When husband and wife team Kim Coleman and Mark Cigolle set out to build themselves a new home, they had one very obvious asset to exploit: an incredible view over the Pacific.

DREAM WEAVER

Above
The low wall provides an anchor for both the bed and the couch, and divides the room without cutting out any of the natural light.

Opposite
While drapes usually shut out the outside world, in this case they divide the bed from the rest of the room and focus attention toward the window.

"You see Santa Monica Bay, a crescent of lights, and stunning sunrises," says Kim Coleman. "And a beautiful set of trees lets filtered light into the house."

Also, the room faces east, which is pretty unusual on the Pacific Coast. The modern house was designed and built to let in the maximum amount of light and to make the most of its ocean-side location.

Transparent and white glass allows sunlight into the house from all sides, and a skylight over the stairs brings yet more light into the center of the house. "What we like about the house is the transition, the changes

Above

The importance of materials is clear: wooden beams, steel beams, and plasterboard are all left exposed which, in a more conventional construction, might have been covered up or papered over.

in the quality of the light from day to night," says Kim.

The view is the reason why the bed is placed not against a back wall but in the center of the room, with the window just a few feet away. Kim and Mark Cigolle constructed a low wall as a bed head, to anchor the bed within the spacious room. Despite the wall, they felt there remained a danger that the bed

Left

Curved walls and spaces rather than doors divide the floor into "rooms"; the bathroom can be seen through the transparent frame in the center of the picture, and door frames are left empty rather than closed up with doors.

Below

The bare plaster that covers most of the walls is broken up at intervals by the gray steel beams and by a brilliant splash of green around the window frame.

would seem to be adrift in the middle of such a large room, so a circle of drapes was installed. The drapes can be drawn around the bed, to create a smaller room within the bedroom.

The silk taffeta curtains also make a dramatic statement, since they are in one of the few bright colors in the room. They also emphasize the bed, and lend a touch of luxury and opulence to the airy space.

Kim and Mark describe the house as a laboratory where they test ideas about light, space, and material.

"In some places there are sheet metal walls, such as around the bathtub, so it's as if the outside surface of the structure has come inside, as if it has rotated and the back of it has come around to the front," says Kim.

The surfaces inside are of smooth plaster and exposed steel beams, both materials that are commonly seen on the exterior, so there's a strong sense of bringing the outside in.

Above

The sheer white
drapes at the
window are from
Creation Baumann,
and provide privacy
while letting in as
much light as
possible.

Kim and Mark didn't use much paint to cover up the natural surfaces. The walls were all given a skim coat of plaster, and most of the plaster was left in its natural color, then sealed with a clear sealer. Paint was used in only a few places. Even then it was mixed with the plaster rather than painted over the top of the plaster. The steel frame was covered with Graphite 2224 paint, and paint color New Leaf

1612 creates a vivid splash of color around a window frame.

With such a plain base to the decoration, it took just a few patterned and colored objects to complete the scheme. The bed cover is by an Italian designer, Paola Lenti, and was chosen because the color echoed that of the steel girders. The pillows, which Kim had already, are by Ligne Rosset. Kim and

Mark designed the bed, incorporating pillows from a couch they had already. They also designed the rest of the furniture and cabinetry, other than the white furniture, which is by Ligne Roset.

Kim added an existing rug, which helped to anchor the bed in its mid-floor position, and to create a patch of bold color within the large space without cluttering it up.

The project took 20 months to finish, though Kim admits they never really complete a project until they move out of it.

"It's actually worked extremely well. The bed is focused toward the view, but there are links to other areas, such as the bathtub and shower, the couch, which is on the back of the low wall, to the rest of the room," she says, adding, "It is lots of fun to live in."

Above

The expanse of flooring reflects light from the ceiling and the large windows.

Above

The fireplace is set in a wall dividing the bedroom and bathroom spaces. Heat is given off in both directions through the inset glass panels.

Opposite

The bathtub is surrounded by sheets of zinc metal, and has a view through the enclosed fireplace to the bedroom beyond.

DESIGN SUMMARY

▶ Concrete surfaces left natural throughout the home

▶ Light and air integral to success of design

▶ Solid steel beams left exposed as part of architectural theme

SIMPLY STYLISH SLEEPER

When interior designers use the word simple, it usually means minimal. In this bedoom case study, the simplicity is warm and appealing, with natural materials setting the style.

In a Californian canyon, actress Ione Skye has turned her home into an oasis of light and calm with the help of leading architect Leonardo Chalupowicz and interior designer David Netto.

The architect and designer completed their work a few years apart, so the creation of Ione's spacious bedroom occurred in two stages, the first of which was the whole-scale conversion of the house by Leonardo.

"It was a post-and-beam house that had been bastardized," he says. "Most of my work was uncovering what used to be there."

The largest room in the house, it was formerly a garage, so Leonardo turned it into a space for living by removing the supporting pillars, which broke up the floor space, and replacing them with two supporting beams. He also added French doors that opened to the yard, high windows around the room, and a tall window to the side of

Opposite

The rope basket is used as a laundry basket and, along with the ribbon stool, provides a focus in the otherwise sparsely furnished room.

Above
The screen behind the bed is made of unstained oak veneer, and the warmth of the natural wood contrasts well with the bare plaster of the walls.

Left
The high windows were added at the conversion stage to maximize the light coming into the former garage.

Opposite
The drawings and paintings on the shelf are by Ione, who is an artist as well as actress; the little girl in the yellow jacket is Ione and David's daughter.

where the bed is now to allow light to flood into the room. The floor was concrete, which remained but was polished and sealed, and the walls were left as unpainted plaster.

After the work was done Ione used the room as an artist's studio, where she could draw and paint. She also used it as an occasional party room. However, she then met interior designer David Netto, who realized the room was being underused. "She was only getting occasional use out of the room," says David. "I suggested she take what was the biggest space in the house and make it into a big, luxurious bedroom for herself.'

Above

The reed window shades allow light to filter in from the garden both day and night, adding to the atmosphere.

He approved of what Leonard had created by taking out the large pillars.

"The way to handle a big space is to make one or two grand gestures that are out of scale, and those big strokes of unpainted wood do the job," he says. "It's a big space, but it does feel cozy when you're inside it, and it's especially nice at night." He installed only low lighting in order to create atmosphere. There are just two ceiling lights and bedside lamps, which keep the pared-down room feeling warm and lived-in. Light was a crucial factor in making the room habitable, and as well as the soft lighting, the window coverings were chosen so that they would let in some light at all times.

"When the shades are down, you're not aware of the glass behind them, so you're not cut off from the outside. There's also a wall of green outside created by the foliage, which is uplit at night, so it can never really be pitch black in the room."

The bed takes pride of place against the main wall, offering a view through the French doors. "It is good to walk in and see the bed ahead of you in any bedroom," says David, "and there is a view of the swimming pool, too, from the bed so it was obvious where the bed had to go."

However, rather than just place the bed against the wall, David sourced two folding light oak screens at B&B Italia (where the bed came from, too) which create the maximum amount of theater. The screens are placed together to make the long backdrop.

A large rug under the bed creates an island to sleep on, along with the bed and the cabinets and the oak screen.

The cabinets were chosen from Cappellini in a shade that David refers to as "that almost-army green because I wanted a strong color."

In such a big room, a pale, pastel color would get lost. As the cabinets are almost the only furniture, they had to be in a strong color.

DESIGN SUMMARY

► Concrete floor surface
► Cabinetry from Italian Cappellini only strong color in room
► Window coverings let light in during daylight hours
► Natural plaster wall surface

The benefit of the huge, natural plaster walls was that they could support substantial pieces of art that would overpower a smaller room. such as the reproduction Mark Rothko painting bought in New York and shipped over.

The minimalist style of the room was partly inspired by two interior designers, Jacques Grange and Lee Mindel, whose work David admires. This room is in the style of Mindel, who is into Scandinavian minimalist design.

The final decorative touch was a long and low shelf for displaying an array of different objects, from paintings and sketches to books and cards. The intention was to provide a light, convenient space where the objects could be changed frequently.

The designer thinks the bedroom's design has stood the test of time. "It looks complete, even with a minimum amount of furniture, and it hasn't been cluttered up or watered down with domesticity. This room is about the life that goes on in it, rather than the stuff that's in it."

CALMING ASIAN INFLUENCE

This is the bedroom space in a compact studio on the water's edge in California. The owner, a professional woman in her thirties, has traveled to the East, and when it came to creating her dream bedroom, the style choice was simple.

Above
The deep red, quilted bedcover brings out the red in all of the other accessories.

Opposite
The bed space is raised up by two steps, with the same bamboo flooring. Rugs offer morning comfort.

The aim was to recreate the peace and tranquility of an Asian-style bedroom, hence the combination of Japanese tansu chests, a polished bamboo floor, and Asian accessories.

"I just wanted it to be peaceful and in harmony with the surroundings," the owner said. "Also, to be warm and comfortable."

The hidden extra in this bedroom space (reached up two small steps from the large living area) is that the bed is positioned so that when you wake up and open your eyes, you are greeted by a stunning view across the bay to San Francisco. When it is sunny, the sun

Above

Dark wood, bamboo flooring and a matchstick blind behind the bed work with the lamp and the cream padded hanging bed head to create an Asian mood.

glinting on the ocean wakes you up to a diamond of a day; when the fog rolls in, the dramatic landscape is intensified.

This neat decorative theme has been achieved in a rented apartment space, and can leave with her should she decide to vacate. The bamboo blind, hanging behind the bamboo pole and the cream canvas headboard pads, the lamps, and the Japanese style chest of drawers adjacent the bed: everything in the studio apartment is portable. Style to go!

Hanging either side of the bed head are small satin pillows. The red features a symbol for love, the green is embroidered with a symbol for a peaceful sleep. The charming silk elephant pillow on the bed is from a range by Jim Thompson and was brought back from Thailand. To repeat the richness of the red coverlet, a red glass vase with faux flowers was chosen. This deep red shade is also dominant in the work of art that hangs above the larger chest of drawers. The color red is also seen in the silk rug, a memento from

DESIGN SUMMARY

► Main floor surfaces are polished bamboo

► Walls are white for lightness

► Red is main accessory color

► Furniture in dark and light wood

► Bedside lamps on dimmers to create mood lighting

► Oriental accessories for calm

► Platform bed well-placed for view

Top
An elephant pillow (for luck) by Jim Thompson.

Above
The work of art above the chest of drawers is a series of panels and fits the space perfectly.

Turkey. The bronze head to the right of the bed is from Thailand, too. A thickly woven basket, filled with books and magazines for bedtime reading, sits on the floor to one side of the bed. Stereo speakers are placed adjacent the lamps and are linked to the main audio system in the living space.

The row of small, built-in small cupboards located above the bed provides more storage for clothes and accessories. Two wardrobes have been built on each side of the passage that leads to the bathroom (not shown), so it doubles as a space to dress.

The success of this sleeping space is in the attention to detail. None of the available space is wasted, which is essential in a studio.

Delicious candy colors for a California girl

revive an existing bedroom.

Left
The clear lamp
base and shade
go with the
transparent chair
in the study area
of the bedroom.

Opposite
Color makes an
impact here on the
walls and is
softened by the
accessories.

SUITE
DREAMS

There was nothing really wrong with the pretty bedroom of a typical young California girl. It was picture perfect, with pale pastel walls, a cozy, wrought-iron daybed and dreamy, floral bed linens. As it turns out, the only problem with the room was that the young child it was designed for was trading tea parties and toys for music and makeup as she transitioned to the teen years. So, Los Angeles-based interior designers Diane Bedford of Bridge Design Studio and Mary Skahill-Brewer of Studio Brewer worked together to come up with a fun, fresh look that transformed the 'pretty in pink' little girl's room into a hip hangout that is sophisticated, but not too serious.

Left
A contemporary fitting provides three levels of light above the bed.

Below
The view through to the dressing and chill-out areas.

Opposite
Colors that might clash elsewhere work well in this teen's dream room.

Above

Soft and shimmery drapery surrounds the platform bed, which has storage underneath it.

The young teen knew just what she wanted, having done her research by reading lots of design magazines and catalogs, so she was familiar with trends and what she wanted to have in the room. She and the designers chose the fabric and colors together.

The room's design success is built upon good-quality items and furnishings designed to transition into adulthood alongside the girl. A platform bed with drawers and a matching nightstand, a desk and hutch unit, as well as a bookcase and an armoire are the important pieces. From there, a scintillating backdrop of raspberry walls punctuated with crisp, white

trim and apple green accents delights the senses and gives the room its playful personality. Metal storage boxes and cabinets add an urban look, while a transparent desk chair and pair of floor-level furry rockers are pure fun. Silk organza drapery panels installed on ceiling mount rods enclose the bed and offer a lighthearted twist on Japanese shoji screens, forming what Diane refers to as "a room within a room." The fabric, in shades of purple and pink, is woven with a metallic thread that shimmers and plays with the light. Not surprisingly, the panels are the girl's favorite feature of her new room.

DESIGN SUMMARY

▶ Main wall surfaces are painted a deep brightpink shade

▶ Cabinets, window surrounds, and closet cupboards painted gloss white

▶ Transparent chair a modern touch

▶ Shimmery fabric surrounds bed

▶ Storage units under the bed

▶ Zany light fittings suit the mood

▶ Cream carpet is hard-wearing

▶ Similar tones in color scheme

Above

Mirror panels on the doors in the dressing area help to light the corner of the room.

Right

A white-painted study unit is a cute contrast to the bright pink wall behind, and the transparent chair updates the look.

This master bedroom is in the same home as the previous case study, and is the refuge of the parents, who have five active children.

COMFORT ZONE

In the master bedroom, the design team took the calm approach, establishing a quiet retreat for the parents. The goal was to create a corner of the home where the couple could kick back, relax, and recharge.

Working with the family on other rooms in the home paid off when the time came to decorate the master bedroom. Designer Diane Bedford and her colleague Mary Skahill-Brewster had worked on the entire house with them, and by the time they got to the master bedroom, the duo had a clear idea of their style and goals.

The homeowner loved fabric, knew what she wanted, and was able to make quick decisions. Throughout the bedroom, variations of sage green and cream, tone-on-tone color in the form of pillows, draperies, and soft upholstery help to present a serene setting.

The starting point was a distinctive carpet, given to the homeowner by her mother-in-law, along with several other Persian rugs which have been used throughout the house. Its bold design is the only patterned feature in the room, and the remainder of the colors were chosen to complement this unusual carpet.

Soft colors are a recurring theme in the house, which is decorated in warm, muted shades of taupe and sage green. In this room, Diane and Mary used painted walls to support the sophisticated mood.

Since the husband frequently uses the master bedroom as a casual workspace, comfort was the key characteristic in choosing the furnishings. A custom-made velvet, upholstered bed frame lined with pillows is the perfect place to sit up and work on a laptop or watch TV. Similarly, a cozy chenilled extra-wide

Above

Bedside lamps are wall-hung to provide more space for flowers and accesories.

Opposite

Custom-made side tables are stained ebony to tone with the antique armoire and chest.

chaise longue in a corner of the room is poised between a window and French door to take advantage of the natural light that comes in here for reading papers or a book.

The magic of the room is found in a masterful mix of carefully chosen design elements that cast the retreat in a warm, enchanting glow. Quilted drapery panels are made of silk, as are the pillow covers and a matelasse coverlet. An exquisite glass chandelier adds Retro glamor that is balanced with a rustic wood chest and an antique armoire. The chandelier is quite something, being constructed from fine crystal tubes in a horizontal pattern. It is a stunning, almost frivolous detail in an otherwise soberly designed room.

"Drop-dead gorgeous chandeliers are hung through the house, and they're all quite different," says Diane.

The room's architecture also plays a strong, supporting role. A dramatic vaulted ceiling adds character without overwhelming the space, thanks to the deep wall color that reins in the scale of the room.

In addition, wood casement windows, French doors, and an outdoor verandah add charming, cottage-quality details.

The only restriction that the architecture placed on the designers were the windows on either side of the bed, which didn't leave quite enough room for full-size end tables, so these were custom made to fit the narrow space. Wall-mounted bedside lamps ensure there is plenty of space on the end table for flowers, photographs, and other personal essentials.

One wall of the room, set aside for beautifully framed photos of family vacations, sporting events, and holiday gatherings, speaks volumes of a close-knit clan.

Left

A corner of the master bedroom is given over to a chaise longue where the owners can relax. Here you can clearly see the detail of the fabric used for the long drapes.

The key is to stay with one color and create contrast with different shades of the same tone. There are about ten types of fabric in this room, including silk, velvet, damask, linen, and mattelasse. The coverlet is particularly textured, as if it were macramé; it looks as if it has been hand-quilted. The lustrous shiny silks and satins create a sense of luxury, while the softer velvet and mattelasse, plus the wool carpet, are comforting.

The combination creates a room that is classic yet contemporary, and fulfills its role as a place for relaxation. "This is a very busy family, so it needs to be a retreat and very peaceful," says Diane.

DESIGN SUMMARY

- Main wall surfaces painted subtle shade of sage green
- Soft and luxurious textures
- All woodwork around windows and doors painted white
- Dark wood side tables, armoire, and blanket chest
- Central chandelier is focal point in lighting plan

Above

The silk drapes are woven with a diamond pattern to give texture and are opened and closed with a long pole rather than pull cords.

The following three bedrooms are each located in an interesting period home, full of character and an elegance of its own.

ITALIANATE STYLE

Above

Two matching Roman blinds add a floral touch to this corner of the room and are in keeping with the small dressing table.

Opposite

The search for a large rug to bring together the entire scheme took a long time but, finally, a decision was made. The blue chair and the trim on the tablecloth match the blue in the carpet.

Absolutely full of storybook appeal and delightful architectural details, the Italian Mediterranean-style residence is the perfect backdrop for an impressive array of antiques and heirlooms acquired by the wife, an avid collector. Built in 1932, the solid home is annotated with leaded glass windows, gracefully arched passages, and beautiful wood floors, all of which contribute to the rich heritage of Pre-war housing.

Though undeniably long on charm, the pretty home was also unarguably short on the one feature that means most to a growing family: space. While working with an architect yielded enough square footage to add a sitting room to the master bedroom, strict zoning laws precluded a major addition to the

structure. This home, however, was worth the sacrifice, so the family opted to make things work within the existing footprint, which is when designer Caroline Baker stepped in.

Her clients, who include a husband, wife, and their three children, were in the process of combining two households into one. The goal was to create a home that included retreats for each person, filled with treasures they loved.

Inspiration for the master bedroom came from an exquisite 18th century Venetian bed. The priceless piece features a hand-carved, gilded frame that surrounds an elaborate oil painting set into the wood panels on the headboard and footboard. The homeowner first fell in love with the piece when she saw it in a magazine ages ago. Years later, she bought the headboard from a family estate and in a serendipitous twist, had the good fortune to find the footboard in an antique shop. Now restored, the museum-worthy bed takes center stage in their master bedroom. The wall color

Above

Shimmering copper fabric reflects one of the colors in the curtains.

Opposite

A glimpse of the sitting room.

was custom matched to the background of the
bed's painted panels. Plush, teal velvet chairs
and a two-toned table skirt edged in burnt
orange Dupioni silk make a comfortable
reading corner near the bed. A beige silk
bedspread adds to the luxe look.

Adjacent to the sleeping area and
accessed through an arch is a small sitting
room, added to expand the bedroom and

create a private retreat within the master suite.
Paying homage to the home's heritage, the
couple wanted the addition to blend
seamlessly with the existing architecture.

Caroline draped the opening in a floral
fabric that picks up colors found in the bed. A
sound-muffling lining enables one person to
watch television or listen to music in the sitting
room without disturbing someone in the

DESIGN SUMMARY

▶ Furniture and furnishings researched to match the period

▶ Wood floors covered by Persian rugs

▶ Drapes are lined to muffle sounds

bedroom. The large windows feature the same floral drapery, and matchstick blinds add light-filtering privacy during daylight. An antique daybed doubles as a comfy sofa and a built-in stone fireplace, though new, was cleverly constructed to reference the home's 20th century design. "The home and the antiques are really the stars," says Caroline. "We created a livable, elegant space for the family."

Above

Soft furnishings on period furniture pieces are the stars in this snug room adjacent the master bedroom.

BOYS' OWN ZONE

Since space was a valued premium, Caroline Baker's first challenge came in the form of creating a bedroom to be shared by the family's two young boys.

"The boys were four years apart and each of them had things that were important to them," says Caroline. "Every child needs a place to display the things they love. My job was to listen to each of them and establish a design that would work."

She began by interviewing them separately to come up with a list of the "must-haves" from both boys. As it turned out, they each had an antique bed brought from the previous home that they wanted to keep in the new space. The beds were the starting point.

The next issue to address was their individual sleeping styles: One boy needed total darkness to comfortably sleep at night, the other liked a bit of light. To solve the problem, Caroline designed a stairstep divider that does the job of separating the room without boxing it in. Staggered panels allow for maximum privacy and darkness for sleeping, but allow light to pass through during the day. Corkboard and shelving added to either side of the divider create a convenient place for a changing display of trophies, awards, artwork and school pennants.

Because the furniture styles were different, the room needed a unifying force. Here, plaid drapery panels do the trick. Installed on metal rods just below the ceiling, the draperies wrap the walls in a swirl of primary colors befitting a boy's room. Smart window shades installed underneath the drapery panels further block the light. The saving grace of the shared room is a dressing area in an alcove beside the sleeping area. Built-in dressers, large closets, and cubbies provide storage for clothing, toys, and games.

"The room has a timeless quality that will see them through the teenage years," says Caroline.

Above
The divider acts as a place for posters and other precious personal items.

Opposite
The color blue is found in the drapes, the bedspread and even the suitcase at the bottom of the antique bed.

GIRL'S OWN ZONE

In the daughter's room, the interior designer's goal was to mix antique pieces that the young girl loved with modern elements to create a pretty room for a teenager.

A collection of beautiful furnishings provided the starting point. In addition to a pair of hand-carved bed frames and an antique armoire, the daughter included a wrought-iron *étagère*, a French bench, and a small mirror among the belongings she treasured.

Caroline's choice of window treatments, striped sherbet-colored silk panels, gives the room a lighthearted lift. Tassel tie-backs and a gold bead trim added to the roller blinds behind the silk drapes add to the fairy-tale feel. Above, a cut-crystal ceiling fixture does double duty by capturing the sun's rays to fill the room with dancing rainbows during daylight hours and providing functional ambient light at night. However, it is the beloved menagerie of stuffed animals, a doll collection, and hand-stitched pillows that create the room's feminine personality.

An alcove with built-in storage and a vanity and dressing area is steps away from the sleeping area. The silk striped fabric was repeated in the Roman shades on the vanity windows to provide a cohesive design element to link the two enchanting spaces.

Opposite
Pale wool rugs are placed strategically on the wood flooring to add a lightness to the area.

Above
An antique French mirror hangs between two fabulous wide windows. Teddy has fallen asleep.

Left
The Roman shades are in the same fabric as the drapes in the bedroom.

WORKING WITH THE PROFESSIONALS

Regardless of the scope of a project of the size of a budget, every homeowner will benefit from a consultation with a design professional. The reason is that few of us are trained to take a three-dimensional approach to the design of our surroundings.

We might know what we want, and what we like, but be less equipped to know the best way to turn that dream into reality. Even more important, design professionals are trained to see the potential of a project.

The challenge is to find a design expert that best suits the scale of your project. If your new bedroom involves major structural changes, a relocation of utilities, or an addition to your home, consider an architect with residential experience. If you plan to remodel within the existing footprint of your current bedroom without significant structural changes, hire a certified bedroom designer. In some cases, it may make sense to consult both types of experts: the architect on style, structural issues, and local codes; and the bedroom designer for expertise on cabinetry, materials, and storage.

Begin the search by asking friends and homeowners in your area for their recommendations. You can also obtain the names of qualified individuals from national organizations that license and certify design professionals, such as The American Institute of Architects (www.aia.org).

Interview several professionals before making a final decision. Look at work that reflects your home's architecture, or is similar to the style of bedroom you want to create.

During the initial consultation, show the professional sketches and photographs that convey your taste, style preference, and design ideas. Also, present a preliminary budget to help guide you toward viable options. At this stage, be prepared to discuss design fees. Is the person willing to negotiate a flat fee for the project, or do they charge an hourly rate? If they bill by the hour, check how much time they expect the project to take. Although design fees vary, estimate the professional's costs to be between 5 and 15 percent of the project's budget.

Do not hesitate to ask questions or to clarify information. Ask the person to walk you through the project from start to finish in order to understand the process. Review drawings and photographs of their previous projects and ask for references. Also ask if you can visit a completed project to evaluate their work before making a decision.

When you have done your homework, it is important to hear what the architect or bedroom designer has to say about your project. Listen to ideas with an open mind and do not be surprised if your vision of the bedroom evolves as you gather information. Professionals approach design from a different perspective than a homeowner; they may point out possibilities you had not considered, or based upon their experience, they may eliminate options. Always keep in mind that the objective is for the design professional to be guided by your vision and your goals, not the other way around. It is your home, your budget, and you are always in control of the project. If the person is not responding to your ideas, or is trying to impose their signature style on you, take that as a cue to move on to the next candidate; communication and a solid working relationship are crucial for success.

Once you have made a decision to hire, set a firm budget, and agreed on terms, your project will proceed to the design phase. The architect or bedroom designer will show you an initial set of plans for review and revision. If you require alterations, now is the time to make them. Even small changes to a final design can be costly and cause delays.

MANAGING THE CONSTRUCTION

While meticulous planning will minimize any problems arising during construction projects, they will not be eliminated entirely. From sorting out small issues, such as cleaning up the site daily, to dealing with more pressing matters, such as extended delays or quality of workmanship, the construction process is layered with details and complexities.

Most state governments have a list of organizations that govern contractors, issue licenses, and set standards of performance. To understand your rights as a consumer, contact the appropriate organization to familiarize yourself with the regulations before hiring a professional to work on your home. Then put a plan of work in place.

OTHER POINTS TO CONSIDER:

▶ Draw up a contract for signature that states the scope of the project, the estimated cost, a payment schedule, and a reasonable time frame for completion. Include details such as how the contractor plans to seal off the work zone, what time workers will arrive each morning, and that they will clean up the site daily.

▶ Read the fine print. Many standard contracts outline terms for settling disputes; some limit the homeowners' ability to take legal action. Make all of the changes before signing the agreement.

▶ Set up a portable file to organize project paperwork and include sections for payments, receipts, and notes of meetings or conversations with the contractor.

▶ Make a list of questions and/or concerns that arise as the construction progresses. Arrange a weekly meeting with the contractor to review the timetable and resolve issues.

▶ When construction is complete, conduct a walk-through to inspect cabinets, surfaces, appliances, lighting, outlets, and plumbing before signing off on the project.

▶ Compile a list of items that need to be addressed and withhold final payment until each matter has been resolved to your complete satisfaction.

INDEX

SOURCES

California Closet Co.
www.calclosets.com

ClosetMaid
www.closetmaid.com

Hammonds Furniture Ltd.
www.hammonds-uk.com

Greystone Home Collection
www.greystonehomecollection.com

Caroline Baker, ASID
Interior Designer
info@carolinebakerdesign.com

Joani Stewart/Montana Ave. Designs,
joanistewart@montanaaveinteriors.com

Diane Bedford/Bridge Design
diane@bridgedesignstudio.com

Nestor Matthews
Matthews Studio
www.matthewsstudio.com

Marisa Solomon, Designer, &
John Reed, Architect
jreedarch@cs.com

Wendy Ann Richens, ASID
Interior Designer
wrichens@richensdesigns.com

Lisa Adams/Troy Adams Design
lisa@troyadamsdesign.com

David Desmond, Interior Designer
ddesmond@daviddesmond.com

Mark Cigolle and Kim Coleman, Architects
kcoleman@usc.edu

Leonardo Chalupowicz, Architect
chalupo@pacbell.net

David Thompson, Architect
Assembledge
www.assembledge.com

ACKNOWLEDGMENTS

I would like to thank my wife, Susan, and my family, Emma Rose, Richard, and Lucy for their support while writing this, my first book.
Thanks also to Hammonds Bedrooms for supplying storage images.
And, of course, thanks to Lynn Bryan for believing in me.

The BookMaker would like to thank Douglas Hill for his superb photography because without it, there would be no book. For his inspirational architecture, thanks go to Nestor Matthews in San Francisco.
To Richard Roberts at Gustavian, thanks.

A huge thank-you to the owners of all the case study bedrooms for letting us photograph their private bedrooms. To the architects and interior designers who worked with them to create these amazing sleeping spaces, thanks, too, for your visions of splendor. Appreciation goes to Michael Giaimo, too, for his Retro vision, and to Cassandra Feist for her Asian experience.

PHOTOGRAPHIC CREDITS:

Pages 8 & 9, Jay Graham; pages 10 & 11, Robin Matthews. Furniture by Gustavian. Page 23, Hammonds Bedrooms; page 33, curtains and fabric by Greystone Fabrics, designed by Claudia Aquino, photographed by James Klotz; page 34, Ray Main/Mainstream Images; page 35, Ray Main/Mainstream Images/Design by William Yeoward; page 37, Ray Main/Mainstream Images; page 40, ceiling design by Janeen Algren Swing, with photograph by Dan Ray; page 45, far right, Hammonds Bedrooms; page 46, Hammonds Bedrooms; page 47, ClosetMaid closet design; page 48, 49, 50: all closet designs by ClosetMaid; page 53, Ray Main/Mainstream Images; page 56, closet designs © 2006 California Closet Co. Inc.; page 57, design by ClosestMaid, and page 63, Sarah Barnard of Sara Barnard Design.
All other photography by Douglas Hill, assisted by Martin Cox.